Windsingers

A Collection of Stories

by

Wyoming Writers

Edited by

Charlotte M. Babcock
Sharon Brondos
Nancy Heyl Ruskowsky

* * * * *

Title and Cover Design by

Marik Turbes

* * * * *

Published by

WYOMING WRITERS, INCORPORATED
IN ASSOCIATION WITH
EAGLE PUBLISHING COMPANY
Cody, Wyoming

Grateful acknowledgment is made to Robert Roripaugh and Dr. Richard Fleck, both of the University of Wyoming, without whose advice and encouragement the choice of entries into this volume might have been altogether impossible.

ISBN No.: 0-917557-01-8

First edition.

CONTENTS

THE MAN WHO LOVED ANTIQUES
by
Debra D. Munn

Walt Sheaffer was a man who loved antiques. This love stemmed from memories of an unusually happy childhood that ended abruptly with his mother's death when he was thirteen.

Through the years Walt kept her memory close by living with the treasures from daily life that she had bequeathed to him. For hours he was content to puff on a Meerschaum pipe, dreaming of his boyhood that had vanished like the smoke swirling away from him. Or he would glance over the sixteen diaries, one for each year since her eighteenth birthday, that his mother had kept until she died suddenly of pneumonia, brought on by the overwork required of her as a farm wife.

Her diaries were bound in red leather imprinted with gold ivy leaves. Out of respect for her memory and to avoid damaging the elegant volumes, Walt had refrained from breaking the leather clasps or the locks which had protected Millie Anderson Sheaffer's secrets for over fifty years. But the unexpected discovery of the key, wedged behind a small drawer in the upper righthand corner of her rolltop desk, he regarded as a sign of permission to look inside.

When he did so, he came to know his mother in a way not possible before. The diaries illuminated the past she had rarely talked about. Walt read about the happy times, such as the ice skating parties when the Grand River froze, and about the sad times, as when her youngest sister, Mary, died of polio. Walt read also about the magical night when his mother met and fell in love with Sam Sheaffer, at a harvest dance in 1910. Sam had drifted into Lansing to hire himself out as a farm laborer; once he saw Millie Anderson, he stayed.

Reading further, Walt was shocked to learn that his parents had married despite the fact Millie's folks disapproved of Sam, clearly regarding him their social inferior. Millie had gone on to record not only the trivialities of her hardworked and, on the surface, unrewarding life, but also her keenly perceptive, bittersweet reactions to family, neighbors, and the interweaving of their lives. The diaries were Millie's special legacy to Walt, a record of the inner life that found no other expression during her thirty-five years.

Only slightly less cherished were his mother's rose-globed bedside lamp (bought during a rare shopping trip to Detroit one winter), a marble-topped table she had inherited from her favorite Aunt Clovis, and the other few pieces of furniture that even poverty could not force Sam to sell after her death.

So Millie's things, now lovingly displayed in Walt's house, were a monument to her, or more exactly, a shrine to a mother he had not understood until after her death.

Walt's wife Flo had never spoken openly of her resentment, born of the feeling that she was usurped in her own home by the ghost of this mother-in-law she had never known. But she did let it be known, to Walt and whoever else would listen, that "For myself, now, I prefer new things. Antiques are too gloomy."

So it was that she was relieved when her husband's retirement brought a change in their living arrangements. At the age of sixty-two, Walt ceased farming to undertake the less onerous work of selling John Deere equipment from his front lawn to younger, hardier farmers. He sold the cows, pigs, and chickens to vacate the barn, which he in turn renovated into his own quarters, separate from the house, which he now entered only to take his meals and to sleep.

Into this new sanctuary he gathered his mother's belongings. He positioned the scratchy horsehair sofa with brass nails against the far wall, adjacent to the rolltop desk. On top of this, he arranged the diaries in order, securing them on either side with the pewter candlestick bookends that had once graced the mantel in his mother's parlor. The rose-globed bedside lamp atop the marble table stood next to his favorite chair, which had been recovered, as he remembered, six times, but always in the same dusky rose chintz.

Walt was comfortable enough in his hideaway in the summer, but the crisp autumn afternoons made him long for the warmth of the potbellied wood stove of childhood, when each morning from late October through early April he had bounded down the stairs like a wild thing, shivering and teeth chattering, possessed by the primal need to get warm.

So it was that one day while driving back from Eaton Rapids, he spied the exact duplicate of this stove in the cobwebbed window of a run-down antique shop.

"How much?" he asked the proprietor, hardly daring to hope that this prize could be his.

"Just four hundred dollars—quite a bargain, I'd say. Though it could use a little polishing up here and there," the shop owner patted the stove proudly.

"I'll take it!" Walt's joy was so intense that he felt as though his lungs might burst.

From the moment of buying the stove, he was obsessed as never before by a demon to recreate the past. He combed the antique and junk shops all over Ingham and Clinton Counties, and whenever he heard about impending estate sales, he went; eager to bid. Soon he began traveling all over Michigan, then down into Indiana sometimes. Once he even drove to Ohio on a quest for an Edison gramophone, which he carried home like a trophy.

Eventually, his equipment business suffered. Flo, who understood nothing about the tractors and harvesters sitting on her front lawn, would have to turn prospective customers away with a "Sorry, he's out antiquing today. Won't you stop by again, please?" And when they did come again, Flo was embarrassed because she had to admit, "No, he's gone again today. But maybe if you call before you come next time . . . ." But in time they stopped coming at all.

When this happened, Flo lit into Walt with pent up fury and humiliation.

"Antiques! Antiques! From morning to night! You're obsessed to the point you can't do your work!"

Walt stared dumbly, not seeing her. Mentally he was exulting over the bargain he had just picked up in Grand Rapids, a Seth Thomas pendulum clock with Westminster chimes. It had cost him only three hundred dollars, and it was rare, too. He was planning to put it over the rolltop desk, where the two shades of oak would complement each other.

Flo continued her protest over the next few weeks, but she got nowhere with Walt. One day, after taking stock of their finances, he canceled his agreement with the equipment manufacturers, and announced quietly but firmly to Flo that their savings alone would be enough to see them through to the end of their days. Flo was angry, but she saw by his face that there was no point in arguing.

And so there might have been enough money, too, if Walt had not continued to dip into their savings to buy more antiques. He bought pie safes, butter churns, chamber pots. He acquired a fancy for cut glass, and soon the growing collection of diamond-like punch bowls and wine goblets demanded a place of honor. To accommodate them, Walt bought a china cabinet reaching from floor to ceiling. His face beamed at the discovery of it. His mother had always longed for such a fine piece as this.

When Flo saw the delivery men moving the huge cabinet into the barn, she rushed out of the kitchen, berating Walt at the top of her lungs. They were not wealthy people; why was he acting as if they were? The china cabinet had cost Walt well over two thousand dollars, money she had intended to use for a trip to California to visit her brother. All the time she ranted, the delivery men, who were really just sixteen-year-old boys, looked shamefacedly back and forth, first to Flo with her eyes bugged out in rage, then at Walt, who stood his ground quietly, showing anger only by the tense workings of his jaw muscles.

The bigger of the two boys finally screwed up his nerve to ask, his voice breaking from embarrassment, "What do we do? Do we leave this here or not?"

"You'll damned well take it back—that's what you'll do! I' not allow my husband to throw all our money away for the sake of a ghost! If you were any sort of man, Walt Sheaffer, you'd face the fact that your mother's been dead for fifty years. And I wish to hell you were dead with her!"

The next second she was hurtled to the ground. Walt stood over her, white hot.

"Put it in the barn. And then you'd better go," he told the boys without looking at them. As quickly as they could move the heavy load, they settled the cabinet into place, then scurried back to the truck and, wordlessly, hurried away.

Flo slowly began picking herself up from the driveway, brushing blood and gravel from her mouth. She gave Walt a look he had never seen before on a human face.

Walt awoke in the darkness to the sound of leaves rustling. The wind made an eerie moan as it vibrated the loose screen. He crept from bed to close the window, then stood listening. The leaves crackling around the yard were unusually noisy, even for such a windy night. And there was a smell that reminded him of the old potbellied stove and of times when he would snuggle near it, between his parents as they told him stories that would have frightened him if they had not been there to chase away the demons of the night. . . .

An orange flickering glow in the sky returned him to the present.

"Flo!" he shouted. Then, turning toward the bed he saw that her place was empty.

"Mother of God!" he whispered, clutching at his heart. He tore down the bedroom stairs, then around to the front of the house, opposite the barn.

A chill swept upward from the pit of his stomach. Paralyzed with horror and disbelief, he was vaguely conscious of two figures running toward the burning barn, trailing lengths of lawn hoses. Then, while Walt continued to stand helplessly, these men were joined by three others, then more and more, until it seemed that all the neighbors for miles around had turned out for some pagan ritual.

Someone was axing through the barn door. Then Walt heard the shouts of the Dawson brothers.

"Stand back! We're going in to see if there's anything to save."

But the Dawsons were forced out in less than a minute, staggering and choking, their arms and faces black. Frank Dawson pitched out the charred remains of what Walt recognized as the rolltop desk.

"That's all. There's nothing else left." Frank coughed up pieces of soot. "And even if there was, it's too hot to go back in."

"All we can do now is make sure that the flames don't reach the house," shouted Bud Adkins, one of the fire department volunteers. "But at least the wind's in our favor tonight, blowing in the opposite direction."

"Anybody know how it started?" Al Dawson wondered.

"Not for certain, but it looks like somebody set it," another neighbor, Matt Wilkins, said, eyeing the men around him cautiously. "I found an empty gasoline can just now, a little ways behind the barn."

"God, no! Who would do such a thing to Walt?" asked Frank.

"Kids, maybe? Hell, I don't know. Walt doesn't have any enemies so far as I know. Although he's always been kind of a queer sort." A hushing began in the assembled group as Walt, still in a daze, approached the burnt rubble Frank Dawson had tried to salvage.

"Walt—if there's anything we can do . . ." Matt faltered. "We'll all help you rebuild your barn as soon as possible. You can count on us. I hope you know that."

Walt remained silent. He stared at all that remained of his mother's desk, then crouched upon his knees for a last, closer look.

"Walt," Matt edged closer to the old man, who was running his hand lovingly over the charred fragment. It was still almost too hot to touch.

"Before you know it, you'll have a new barn and even more antiques than before. Just you wait, you'll see." Matt sounded as if he were addressing a child instead of a man old enough to be his father.

Walt finally looked up. "There'll be no more antiques," he said, so low they could barely understand him.

An awkward pause followed, before Al Dawson drew Matt away. "Leave him alone. There's nothing anybody can do for him right now."

"Say, where's Flo? Anybody seen her?" asked Frank.

Walt spoke again, in the same quiet voice. "She's not here."

"Where is she then?"

Walt could not answer, but only shook his head from side to side. His soul sickening, he watched the barn shudder as if in agony before its roof caved in, shooting sparks and red-hot debris up into the blackness. For one awful second the interior gaped open where the roof and part of the outside wall had been; he saw the incandescent glow of the china cabinet before it exploded into fiery fragments.

But the cruelest torture for Walt was the sight of his mother's diaries scattered roughly across the floor, now recognizable as books only by their singed covers curling backwards into ash.

Author note. Born in Amarillo, Texas, Debra D. Munn holds a B.A. in telecommunications from Texas Tech and worked as a radio newscaster. She returned to Texas Tech for an M.A. in English. In 1982 she received a Ph.D. in American literature from Florida State University. She is an instructor of English and American literature at Northwest Community College in Powell, WY, and has published two articles in American literature journals.

HARRY'S CRAZY MOTHER
by
Maurine Moore

She moved into our neighborhood the same year I started junior high and no one seemed to know much about her. She had a son my age named Harry, so I figured she'd been married some time or other, but she never said if she'd been married or divorced.

Harry used to ditch school all the time without getting caught. I asked him how he did it and he said his mom wrote excuses for him. Seems she had the idea school wasn't a prison and if somebody wanted to take off and just goof around for a day or two, it was okay. I always got in trouble if I ditched.

Harry's mom taught school for a while. My sister took a high school class from her and she'd come home and tell us about the wild things they talked about . . . sex or anything else, even though the class was history and wasn't supposed to be interesting.

My folks got pretty uptight about it so my sister didn't tell us much after the first few weeks. She always did her homework, though, and it was one of the few classes she ever got good grades in. The other kids seemed to enjoy it as much as Sis did. She told me one day she got there a little late and there was nowhere to sit. Seems the other kids had been ditching other classes to come to hers. It made some of the teachers mad and they complained to Mr. Troy, the principal. He tried to put a stop to it, but they came in anyway and she never reported them.

I was looking forward to taking a class from her when I got to high school, but a lot of the parents must have felt the same way mine did because she taught for two or three years and never got her contract renewed again. It was probably just as well, but I was disappointed.

Nobody could figure out how she made a living after that. One rumor was that she wrote short stories and sold them to magazines. My mom and Mrs. Bundy, the widow who lived next door, were hopping mad one day because they read a story in a romance magazine in which a lot of the characters sounded familiar. They were going to sue her to put a stop to it, but if Harry's mom wrote it she used another name, so they never could prove anything.

My mother usually didn't buy that type of magazine so I asked her how she happened to see the story in the first place. She looked embarrassed and told me to go wash my hands for dinner, so I never asked her about it again.

One day when we first started high school Harry and I walked home together. My folks didn't like me to hang out with Harry, but school had been dismissed early that day for a teacher's meeting or something, so when he invited me in I figured I could still get home on time and no one would know I'd been there. Besides, I was curious to see the inside of the place.

The rug was threadbare, but there was a shiny new piano in the living room. Harry's mom had gotten it for him the day before as a surprise when it wasn't his birthday or anything. I hadn't realized Harry was the one who played it; I always thought it was his mom because the music I heard sometimes when I passed their house was the type most grown-ups preferred. She didn't make him practice if he didn't want to, either. It sounded crazy to me that someone would buy a piano just for fun.

The delicious smell I noticed when I walked into their house that day was coming from some tiny chicken legs she had just baked. I ate three or four of them before Harry told me they were really chicken wings his mom had cut up to look like little legs. I didn't believe him until he showed me how she did it, then I felt kinda funny because I don't like chicken wings and never ate them. But they tasted all right and we were laughing and talking by then so I never let on how I didn't care for them. In fact, I ate a few more just to make her feel good.

She was a pretty woman, I guess, if someone that old could still qualify. She had long, shiny hair and a nice figure. I noticed whenever she was around other women she was the one you looked at, so she must have been fairly attractive.

Harry's uncle came to visit while I was there. Someone was always dropping in to see them, young or old, men or women, it didn't seem to matter. Mrs. Bundy, whose house was between ours and Harry's told mom she never could keep track of the cars that parked out front. He stayed just a few minutes. He said he'd gotten a new car and wanted to brighten up her neighbor's day by giving her something to talk about. I didn't understand what he meant, but Harry and his mom and uncle were still laughing when he left.

Harry began to complain to his mom about his French teacher and I backed him up because I had the same one and she was a real dragon. Harry said she was so stupid he knew more than she did and he couldn't stand to sit and listen to her for an hour every day. The amazing thing was that his mom agreed with everything he said. She sure spoiled him. If I ever complained to my folks about a teacher they just told me to shut up and behave myself.

After we had discussed it for a while, though, she said a funny thing. She said school shouldn't be a prison for the teachers either; they should be able to enjoy themselves and not dread having to go every day. That was the craziest thing I'd ever heard. I always figured teachers were like wardens whose job it was to torment us kids. It had never occurred to me that they might not like being there any more than we did. After that, whenever I saw a teacher looking unhappy or stuck at a desk grading papers I remembered what she'd said. Harry didn't seem to have any more trouble in French after that. He told me later he'd lucked out and gotten an "A".

Harry was an expert at that—getting good grades, I mean. He was big and good looking and quiet and everybody liked him, especially his teachers. Besides, after he got into high school he hardly ever cut classes any more. The dumb cluck could have been gone half the time and his mother would have written excuses for him, but he said he missed his friends when he was gone so he didn't like to take off too often. He skipped school one day, though, and Mr. Troy caught him and told him he couldn't get back in unless his mom came with him.

The next day I got an earache and went in during first period to see the nurse. Her office was right next to the principal's and while I was waiting for her to examine me Harry and his mom came to talk to Mr. Troy about Harry getting back into school. They all started out being real polite, but when Troy said if he caught Harry ditching again he'd expel him, his mom got real mad and told him to go jump in the lake because Dr. White would give Harry an excuse any time she asked him to and then what was he going to do about it?

Dr. White would have done it, too. Everyone in town knew he was sweet on Harry's mom and came around to see her all the time. Rumor had it he wanted to marry her but she said she didn't want to break up a beautiful friendship. She was a weird one, all right. Most women would have jumped at the chance to marry a nice rich guy like Dr. White.

Anyway, after Mr. Troy and Harry's mother got through yelling at each other they walked out of his office and didn't speak to anyone. Harry was out of school quite a lot for a while after that, but nothing seemed to come of it and soon he was there every day. Nobody ever seemed to stay mad at Harry . . . not even old man Troy.

I got mad at him once, though. In fact, I was so mad, if he hadn't been a lot bigger than I was, I would have beaten him up. We both went out for track our sophomore year and Harry was outstanding. He broke every record the school had for broadjumping during practice. The coach was so happy he smiled all the time and said when Harry got to be a senior he would be breaking every record in the state.

One day while we were practicing, though, Harry sprained his wrist so bad he couldn't play his stupid piano. He could run and jump, but he couldn't play the piano . . . so he quit track! The coach didn't understand why and went to talk to his mom about it. I was standing around the day he was there. He was really mad when he went in, but when he finally left he didn't look too unhappy. I asked him what had happened and he mumbled something about how everyone should get to do their own thing.

I was still mad, though, because if Harry had stayed on the team we would have won state every year. Each time I went by his house and heard the racket he made with that piano I'd get mad all over again. He was so stupid. If he'd stayed with track he could probably have gotten a scholarship.

I didn't stay mad at him too long then either, because he'd come to my house a lot of times after a big snow and help me shovel off our walks after he had finished theirs. He dug my mom and Mrs. Bundy out of a snowdrift one day when they were in a big hurry to get somewhere, and wouldn't take any money for it. He said they were such nice neighbors he considered it a privilege to help them when he could.

After that Mom didn't object so much when I hung around with him. I was sure glad because Harry had a lot of good-looking chics who liked him. I got dates with cool girls I wouldn't have had a chance with if I hadn't been Harry's friend.

He didn't date much, though, because he had a job. He said he was trying to save enough money to go to college. It served him right since he'd quit track and fouled up his chances for a track scholarship. But I used to wish he had more time to mess around because no matter what we did it was more fun if Harry was there.

He lucked out, too, for in our senior year he got to be class valedictorian and won a scholarship after all. He gave a speech the night we graduated. I got the award for best school attendance so I was right beside Harry on the stage and could see everything that went on. His mom cried the whole time he was talking . . . the first time in my life I'd ever seen anyone cry and look happy at the same time. But you couldn't blame her too much. Harry stood right there in front of all those people and told them what a wonderful mother she was and how she deserved all the credit for his success.

Afterwards the newspapers took pictures and everyone got excited, even Mr. Troy. He ran around and smiled during the whole thing. We had a party afterwards and although it has been ten years, it is still the best party I've ever been to. Harry and I had dates with the two neatest girls in school. I don't remember everything that happened, but we didn't get home until almost time for breakfast the next morning. Every time I think about that night I get a happy feeling.

After that summer I lost track of Harry. We went to different colleges and I heard later he'd gotten married and moved to Kansas City where he was doing real well. His mom moved away, too, about the time he finished school. Evidently she was somewhere close by where she could see Harry and his family.

Recently, when I was back home for a visit with my folks, Mrs. Bundy came over to chat. She had been to Kansas City the week before and dropped in on Harry's mom. She caught her teaching her two little grandchildren how to shoot craps. She claimed she was really teaching them arithmetic; but Mrs. Bundy was scandalized, and so was my mom when she told her about it. I had to walk out of the room for a minute so they wouldn't see me smile.

In my job I travel a lot and sometimes I go to Kansas City. Maybe the next time I'm there I'll look up that crazy mother of Harry's and stop in for a visit. She might be baking some of those delicious little chicken legs. Her neighbors won't recognize my car and I'll bet they will wonder who's there this time.

Author note. *Maurine Moore is a Graphological Consultant who resides in Cheyenne, Wyoming. For many years she has written as an avocation and been published extensively in legal and graphological journals.*

In 1982 in her first attempt at writing fiction she won first place in the national American Mother's Literary Contest.

Moore has been a resident of Wyoming for 25 years.

SAMSON
by
Robert O.H. Perry

Samson was a boar pig, and that summer of '52 he had more trouble than any one beast could be expected to handle by himself. Billy and I had been silently standing outside his improvised jail, contemplating the wreck of the county's finest Berkshire boar.

He *was* a mess. His legs were swollen and scratched, with dried smears of blood here and there, and it smelled as if he had had nervous diarrhea. Worst of all, he was skinny!

"Mercy!" I exclaimed. "Don't you feed him?" Still silently, Billy pointed to the full feedpan and waterbucket, untouched. Beyond them, the poor old pig slept on in spite of my voice.

I spoke severely. "What's the matter with you, Samson? Don't you know there's a war on? Every pig must do his duty if we're going to lick the Commies."

"Police action," said Billy. I ignored him. So did Samson. His ear twitched a little, but he was engrossed, dedicated to the sleep of escape from whatever was bothering him.

Billy said, "Watch this," and rattled a slat almost imperceptibly. Samson convulsed. All the mere 400 pounds of his present self flexed upward in an incredible display of sheer terror. He twisted his feet underneath himself in midair and his hind trotters had already gone through the motions of two great leaps before ever they touched the round concrete floor of the corn crib. When they did, he slid like a cat on linoleum, throwing clouds of bright golden straw into the air. Squealing louder than the "Slow But Willing," our local freight train, the boar twirled around the pen, dumping the feedpan and knocking his waterbucket into a cocked hat of tin.

"Samson!" Billy hollered. "Hey, you—Samson!" Foolishly, I thought, he waved his hat (made of straw). It caught Samson's rolling eyes and he calmed almost immediately, slowing down and finally standing in the middle of the pen with trembling legs and heaving sides. Whatever he was afraid of—if anything—it wasn't people.

"He's crazy," I declared.

"Yeah," said Billy.

With the early summer sun soaking our backs, we pondered a

while in glum foreboding. Somewhere a chicken was clucking mournfully. Samson stared back at us.

Dark and lean, as only a beanpole with a boot brush atop it could be, Billy Simpson is a home grown local farmer, while I am a city slicker retread, buying out my wife's folks after I retired from the Navy. As I am short and round and bald, some say we look like Mutt and Jeff when they see us together—people say so, I mean.

Samson didn't say anything. He just came over and pressed against the wall next to Billy, as if for comforting. And old "Hardhearted Hank," he opened the gate and reached over the partition to scratch his bristles with a sound like striking matches.

He said, "Ever since I got him, he's been a pet. Before he got old enough so I made them stop, the kids used to ride him."

Like most farmers, Billy firmly believes an unaltered male animal is potentially dangerous. But that conviction doesn't stop some farmers from being fond of some animals, so long as nobody much knows about it. ". . . I just hate to send him off to market," he finished.

"It's not a cheerful thought," I agreed. "But he's no good to you or himself that way. He's so miserable that if you could only ask him, he'd probably rather be a 'whump' on the grinder."

"Any hot dogs they made out of him would probably give you nervous indigestion, but I guess that's not my problem. Them as buy factory vittles deserve what they get," pronounced Billy.

"Yeah. Well . . . anyway," I said.

"Yeah. . . . Anyway."

It had all begun—for me at least—with Billy's voice on the hand-cranked telephone. "Say, you old bore, you wouldn't still be wanting to trade off any of those young boars, would you? The ones Bertha and Wanda farrowed after Samson came to call are the ones I had in mind."

There were several clicks along the party line as various neighbors hung up again.

"Well, a couple," I replied cautiously. Then a happy thought nudged me and I went on, "Of course, the no-good ones sold right away, so the litters have been culled down to just the best ones left, saved back for my best neighbors."

There was an amused snort from Billy, and I thought perhaps another sound, of muffled misery.

At dinnertime, as everyone was all too well aware, nobody on this line made a noon call—however dull—without being fully auditioned by the community critic, a certain Gustav Gustavsson. And Gus, to my profit, had bought three young boars from me a while back. What's more, he paid cash!

Down at the crowded drugstore coffee shop, with the fans whop-whopping over the dark walnut booths and mirror-backed soda fountain, I had gotten a big boot out of telling Billy about the now orphaned moths that had fluttered out of the old man's antique wallet. He'd said no doubt the moths had circled our heads—singing a Norwegian dirge.

The story had gotten around at flank speed, because the overflowing cream can of the jest was that Old Gus had raised Samson himself, and sold him as a weaner to Billy. Later, of course, he could have thrashed himself when Samson and his get started winning all the fairs and his sons sold for breeding stock themselves. But Gus had been so nasty over the terms of the original sale that Billy never would sell the boar back to him, or even a breeding service, let alone one of Samson's sons.

Naturally, I'd asked Billy first if it was all right for *me* to sell Gus one of mine, before somebody else did, and he'd just grinned like a jack-o-lantern and suggested, "Make him squeal."

And I had. We'd haggled like the Korean negotiators at Panmunjon. In the end, Old Gus was so cheap he wouldn't meet my price on the good ones, and had settled for second best.

So now we savored the outpouring of mute anguish for a while before I asked Billy, "What's wrong with Samson? I thought the firm of Samson and Simpson had the piggin' business in the bag for the next few years."

"Yep," said Billy. "So did I. But there's something come over Samson and I can't figure it out."

Now—if it had been up to me, I never would have let on when Gus could hear about my troubles, but Billy went on, "I guess you could say that Samson seems to be downright bored with the sows these days." He just couldn't resist, never could.

I let the silence lengthen, ominously, this time. But except for occasional lapses such as these, Billy wasn't a bad neighbor—one of the best, in fact. So I let the tail go with the hide.

"Well, suppose I rattle over to your place so we can discuss it in private." I leaned on the last two words a little, but there still was no click on the line. That old man was tough!

"Wouldn't want to put you out any," said Billy.

"No trouble," I replied. "Just now the Missus is finishing up the dishes with a 'why don't you' look in her eye that I mightily distrust. Wouldn't mind a bit coming over on business." I picked the damp dishtowel off my head and repeated, "No trouble at all."

When I got to Billy's he was waiting for me in the yard with a bemused expression and a bucket of food scraps. He handed the latter to me.

"You won't believe it," he hollered over a vociferous dog ensemble, "but it's a fact. Soon as you hung up, Old Gus called and mentioned *he* had some business to discuss. 'Anytime,' I told him, 'but I won't be going out to the field for a while because I have other company coming anyway,' 'I know it,' he came right out with. But, nope, *he* wants to talk private-like."

I acquired the bemused expression as well as the scraps. "Aside from the bare-faced nerve, that's not like him. Unless maybe he figures to put a *real* raunchy one over on you and don't want witnesses. Unless he likes a fair gathering so he's got a choice of victims to skin."

"Maybe he just wants to gloat over Samson's and my misfortunes."

"He likes witnesses for that," I pointed out.

We considered the possibilities while slopping through a couple of barn lots, scattering poultry and keeping a respectful fence away from a high headed, brisk looking Jersey bull and his apparent sidekick, a malevolent old gander.

Billy pointed to as fine a set of young pigs as a farmer could yearn for, and said, "Those are Samson's get, but I already sold all the breedable boars and these're the last he'll likely ever sire. None of the sows he's been with seem to be bred back. Poor Samson. Ain't nothing left of him but eyeballs and floppy tail."

Finally we toiled up toward a silo-type wire corn crib, built in '49, he said, but twisted into uselessness the next year by a freak wind. The conical roof had mostly blown off, and the top half of the wire part was bent and folded over on one side so that its rim was about six or seven feet from the ground. The bottom portion, however, was four or five feet high and reinforced by wooden slats.

"Is this where you're keeping him?" I exclaimed. "How come no handcuffs or armed guards? Sweet suffering sassafras! I'd be unsociable, too, if you treated me this way."

"Well, at least it's holding him so far," said Bill uncomfortably. "Oh, I tried to keep him in with the sows all right, but he just kept getting out. Darn near every morning he'd be on my front porch, looking a whole lot like you did the morning after the last Saturday night dance." He gazed calmly down at my glare and gobble. "Finally got so bad I actually had to set the dogs on him to get him back into a pen—any pen. He'd mess himself up something awful getting out of things, but somehow he did get out, no matter what."

"A real escapologist, huh?"

"A *Houdini*, you mean. You said it. Sometimes in the early mornings I'd hear him squealing fit to tear up a whole graveyard, but by the time I'd get out of the house, he'd be out of the hog lot, and no sign of why."

We arrived at the corn crib and viewed its prisoner.

And that's when Billy put Samson through his paces with the slat rattling. I guess he *had* to show me. I wouldn't have believed it otherwise.

Billy came over to my place after supper. "You'll never guess," he said. "Old Gus wants to buy Samson!"

"No! He's crazy as a pet coon!"

Huh-uh, he's crazy like a fox. *I* can't figure why he wants a non-breeding boar, but somehow *he* sees some advantage in the deal."

"He offer a good price?"

"Well, that's what's got me going. It's not near enough if Samson were in his prime, but it's 'way too much the way he is now."

"That *is* strange. Old Gus is as tight as a bull's rear end in fly season. He's got to be figuring that all his past failures came from offering so low a price that you were insulted."

"Well, they were. 'Course, he might have some trick up his sleeve. Anyway, just to spite him, I told him I'd think about it. But what *we're* going to think on, real hard, is what it is about Samson that he might know that we don't."

"I've already thought myself into circles. I'm tired of meeting myself."

"Don't blame you. But think harder. I can't hang fire *too* long—those sows are filling their flanks full of fat, not pigs, 'cause I was too dumb to save back a replacement for Samson. I have to have the money I'll get for Samson if I'm going to buy another good boar."

He didn't have to say it: borrowing was out of the question. I knew that barely scabbed over memories of near foreclosure during the Depression were hobbling through his mind. It had taken a world war to get Billy out of debt for the first time in his life. A really bad crop, TB in the milk cows, a barn fire, even the loss of several pig litters in a row could start him into a downward spiral again.

He sighed. "Wish I had Old Gus's money and he had a feather stuck in him—we'd both be tickled then."

I fell off the wagon again that next Saturday night. The wife got so mad she caught a ride home from the dance with neighbors. I guess my troubles aren't near as bad as Samson's were, but there *is* a tie-in.

They say I was drunk as a waltzing piss ant, but I wouldn't know. The first thing I remember was a screech as if somebody goosed an aircraft carrier, followed up by feeding a few hundred rolls of wire fencing into its propellers.

I sat stark upright, realizing I had passed out in the seat of my car, and the engine was still running. I fumbled to shut it off, and then the seeming naval catastrophe got worse sounding than ever. When the scenic stuff stopped spinning like Gus's wallet moths, I used my hands as tugboats to focus my face on the commotion.

It was just dawn, and through a magenta mist, I saw that I had· dwindled to a stop about opposite Billy Simpson's farmyard. The bent over wire corn crib where Samson was incarcerated seemed to be heaving and keening; and over at the house, the lights were on and Billy was coming out the back door, blue striped pajamas flapping on his stork-like peripherals, his hands busy stuffing shells into a shotgun. He snapped it together and cleared the first barnyard fence like a giraffe with the heelflies after it as I got him lined up in my blurry vision. His bare feet churning through mud and manure, he hurtled recumbent cows as he encountered them and was across the first lot and squaring up to the next fence before I even made a move.

Then, forgetting all about the fact that I was dead and better buried, I crawled out of the car and legged it across the ditch, negotiating the barbed wire fence, to the sorrow of my best dancing pants and severe risk to the next generation.

Billy and I were both in the final lot and closing in on the corn crib when it erupted. Shrieking, scrambling and yammering shrilly, Samson rose above the slatted part of the crib like a repulsive Venus from wood laden foam. His front feet thrashed about in the loose hanging top part for maybe a year or so, and then the remaining portions of the roof bounced and bonged and finally crashed away in separate panels as Samson's weight and woe bore the whole structure to the ground. His screams punctuated by wires twanging and popping, Samson writhed and slithered toward freedom, dragging his problems right along behind him. As if it were an inappropriate afterbirth, there now emerged—firmly attached to the pig's stretched out tail—the malevolent old gander I had seen the other day! What's more, even with his feet dragging limply and wings balanced widely on the bounding crib wire, the gander seemed to be grinning evilly with his clenched beak.

As the boar reached the ground and attempted to engulf the horizon, the goose released his tail with an audible snap. Neck leveled out low, he hissed triumphantly at the world in general. Then, flapping mightly, with his feet dancing smoothly along and his outstretched neck a-weaving, that gander was after Samson like a hungry God after sinners, pinching delightedly at such personal and private parts of the hapless beast's anatomy as were easily available from such a strategic position. All of a sudden, I knew why Samson twirled when frightened.

Now I saw it—saw it with my own eyes! Samson *jumped* the feedlot fence! I know pigs don't jump. I have no idea how he did it. But he did. He had to, so he did.

The gander flapped with a little extra effort and achieved the top rail of the fence. There he balanced, folding his wings and twisting his long neck into artfully sinuous curves as he surveyed his victim with first one eye and then the other. He gabbled softly to himself and I swear he was smiling still.

Below him in the small lot, Samson churned round and round, pausing at regular points of the compass to "do a dervish." His wailing never ceased, and small blame to him. Who would guess and fear better than he what that sadist's next atrocity might be?

The goose made up his mind and had half raised his wings to launch himself like the Luftwaffe when the shotgun spoke—with authority. *That* brought him down to earth—and then some! Billy said later it was like a tornado getting amongst the Monday washline.

As the last frazzled feather settled, Billy walked deliberately over to the still quivering gander. Judiciously, he aimed—at the head, so as to save the meat. Guess he could have chopped it off, but the ax was back in the barn. Besides, I think he wanted the satisfaction of blowing the evil plumb away. *I* would have.

Samson was still whining a little, and trying to root his way under a corner of the lot. The second shot started him squealing again, and it looked as if he were actually going to lift the cornerpost and squeeze into the next pen. But his tribulations were over now, if only we could have told him so.

I cleared my abused throat and talked to Billy instead. "Suppose that'll be fit to eat?"

Billy was preoccupied, nudging the goose with a filthy toe. Looking more storklike than ever, he balanced on one foot in the dawn light, his pajamas flapping in the early breeze, the other foot fanned out in a large white wing.

I went on, "I'll bet Samson'll be his old self again in no time, now." Thinking it over, "Been having any trouble with your bull lately?"

Billy said, obliquely, "You and I have some plotting to do."

I just stared at him.

Impatiently, he assessed my condition and condescended to explain. "About a week after he bought those boars from you, guess who came over here and swapped off that gander? On purpose!"

Oh, my . . . I started making those gobbling sounds again. Then we drew breath together and recited grimly: "Old Gus Gustavsson!"

Author note. *Robert O.H. Perry is the pen name used by Judy R. Johnson. Born in Hollywood, California, she now lives near Sundance, Wyoming and is devoted to her writing. She intends to specialize in science fiction.*

A WHOLE BANANA TASTES
LIKE RAW CHALK
by
Betty Evenson

I started to school in 1915 when we lived at Plum Grove Farm near Harveyville, Kansas. That was the year that Verley Henderson was my friend.

She sat across the aisle from me at District Number 7 Rural School. There were twenty-one pupils in all grades, so I had a lot of time to myself. I went through the primer the first week and the first grade reader on the following Monday. The so-called busy work which harried teachers gave precocious beginners in those days bored me. I hated to handle clay because it got stuck under my fingernails in gritty gray streaks. Making numbers or designs out of various length bright-colored sticks was repetitious and I found stringing wooden beads on a heavy yellow cord very monotonous.

Verley was in the third grade. She was a stodgy child who did not talk much, but she allowed me to read her textbooks and to do her arithmetic problems for her. I was grateful because the third reader was more interesting than the first; and there was a geography book with wonderful maps that I pored over by the hour so that I was often one of the first to find the places when we had Geography Matches on Friday afternoons.

I was impressed, too, by Verley's high standard of living. We often ate lunch together and she carried hers in a little leather case made especially to hold lunches; not in a tin syrup pail with holes punched in the lid like we Foster kids used. Her box had compartments the proper size for fruit and cake; the sandwiches were made with bakery bread so that they were neatly rectangular; and she often had a whole banana, just for herself.

Once in a great while when relatives came to visit and brought us treats from town, we had bananas at Plum Grove Farm, but they were never eaten in the hand like an apple. They were put into Jello or sliced over custard pudding.

I was thrilled when Verley asked me to stay all night with her at the Henderson Farm and was so excited that I couldn't eat my oatmeal the morning of the much anticipated day. Dotty Dimple, Ellen's pet hen who slept on the edge of the wood box behind the kitchen stove had laid an egg the day before and it was Evelyn's turn to have it fried for breakfast. Usually I watched with vicarious appreciation as one of my sisters ate; but today I scarcely noticed and didn't even bother to count on my fingers how many days it would be before it was my turn to have the egg.

Verley was an only child and her father called for her after school every day in a shiny black buggy. I felt extremely elegant as I climbed up on the high seat beside her and turned to wave condescendingly to my brother and sisters plodding off by foot on the two mile trek toward Plum Grove Farm.

As we jogged along, Verley's father did not say a word and I stole a puzzled glance at him. My idea of fathers, gained from observing my own daddy, was that they were always jovial and interested in anything children had to say. I kept waiting for Mr. Henderson to ask me my name or how I liked school or to tell us something about the countryside and animals we were passing; or even maybe, considering how rich they were, to pull a bag of candy out of his pocket and let us guess what was in it before he offered it to us.

But he did not once glance at me, nor at Verley. He just drove, with his face set in a heavy scowl. Verley did not speak a word either. Once I exclaimed, "Oh, look at that beautiful tree!" as we passed close to a huge scarlet maple whose fall foliage was a brilliant blaze in the afternoon sunshine.

There was no response, so I turned directly to Verley and said "I love the autumn, don't you?"

"It's all right," she answered unenthusiastically and her father cleared his throat menacingly and spat over the buggy wheel into the dusty road.

I was quiet after that, contenting myself by trying to remember the words to a poem by George Cooper that was on page forty-two of Verley's third reader:

"October gave a party,
The leaves by hundreds came
The ashes, oaks and maples
And those of every name."

I wanted to recite it to them, but decided they wouldn't enjoy it.

Mrs. Henderson was a chunky little woman with thick pudgy hands and a habit of leaning close to you when she talked, which was very unpleasant because her breath smelled like rotting sweet corn. She made quite a fuss over me, saying that Verley had talked so much about me . . . I tried to imagine Verley talking so much about anybody.

Verley did not have to do any chores, not even feed the chickens or carry the wood, so we stayed in the kitchen while Mrs. Henderson started to prepare supper. When I offered to set the table she said

"Well, ain't that nice and how can a little girl like you set the table?" doing it herself, meanwhile, with brisk movements.

"I set the table all the time at home, and help do the dishes, too," I boasted.

Mrs. Henderson swooped over me like a blast from an open silo and chucked me under the chin. "Now, you just don't worry your head with the work. You and Verley go in the other room and play."

We went into the parlor, which smelled musty. There was an enormous leather sofa and a library table with thick carved legs. Verley said "What shall we play?"

Verley's dolls were upstairs and, anyhow, I thought playing with dolls was pretty much a last resort. Now, paper dolls, that was different. Evelyn and Jane and I cut whole families out of the catalogs and we had little villages with several households and invented situations full of drama and excitement. But Verley had only the store bought paper dolls with dresses that you could put on and take off, fastened with little tabs over the shoulder and at the hipline. All you could do with them was put on one dress after another, which was not very interesting. I laid the paper dolls back into their cardboard shoe box.

"We could play Jack, if we had a piece of paper and pencils," I suggested.

"The only pencil I have is at school," Verley demurred. "Daddy won't let me use his, and anyhow there isn't any paper to waste. Just the tablet that Mama has for letter writing and we can't use that for playing."

I was astounded at this. I couldn't imagine a father denying the use of a writing implement to his child; and apparently the Hendersons had never realized the full potential of the backs of used envelopes and brown paper sacks from the grocery store. Kate even used the pink mottled paper that sausage came wrapped in when she wrote her poetry, although the slick finish and the grease made the poems hard to read.

"Then let's play 'I'm thinking of a word that rhymes with . . .'" I suggested. Verley looked completely blank, but after a great deal of explanation on my part she consented to try. She couldn't come up with any questions to ask me, so I let her think of a word. I never did guess it because she chose taffy to rhyme with candy.

"But Verley, don't you see it would have to be *dandy* or *handy* or *sandy*?"

"I don't see why," Verley insisted. "Taffy and candy are certainly alike."

She was insulted after that and refused to cooperate when I suggested we sing the multiplication tables, which we did to the tune of Yankee Doodle every night at our house after supper, for Evelyn's sake, because she was having trouble with the sevens. Or we could recite the states and their capitals, which was what Kate was studying in sixth grade geography.

Verley just shook her head sullenly and went back to the paper dolls, putting a ruffled blue party dress on and off blonde Clara Beth—over and over until she broke one of the tabs off.

At supper there were napkins at each place and a silver spoon holder in the center of the table. We had baked potatoes which I had never tasted before, and cooked pears and a huge thick frosted chocolate layer cake. I was impressed and thought that the Hendersons had gone to a lot of trouble to fix a company dinner because I was there, but Verley told me later that they always had suppers like that. I ventured timidly to tell Mrs. Henderson that I thought the food was delicious, but she ignored me and I soon realized that she, like Verley, did not talk when the man of the house was present.

He ate in stony silence interrupted only by the scraping of silver against china and the great sighs he heaved every now and then as he paused to chew before taking another bite. His wife watched him anxiously, rising to hurry toward him when the supply was getting low with replacements of biscuits, ham, or cabbage slaw.

When he finished eating he went into the parlor and we women spoke in hushed tones while we did the dishes and tidied the kitchen. While Mrs. Henderson was out on the back porch shaking the tablecloth, I whispered to Verley. "Doesn't your Daddy ever talk to anybody?" My voice carried better than I intended and Mrs. Henderson answered crisply as she came back into the room.

"Of course he talks. He just doesn't like to be bothered with children chattering."

I felt the reproof in Mrs. Henderson's voice blow over me in a chilling stream and the two pieces of chocolate cake that had tasted so good suddenly lay heavy on my stomach.

When the kitchen was cleaned up there wasn't anything else to do and I was glad when Mrs. Henderson told us it was bedtime. We were crouched in the living room behind the stove and she leaned down to say in a fetid whisper, with her hand to one side of her mouth to insure even greater privacy for the burly man reading his paper under the hissing gasoline table lamp.

"Now you girls be sure to go OUT before you go to bed."

She spoke the phrase shamefacedly and we hung our heads and slunk out the back door like two little sinners bent on committing a crime. At home we regarded the bodily functions rather casually and often when it was snowing or muddy, Daddy would grab a girl under either arm and take us squealing down the path to the outhouse and wait outside, singing church hymns lustily until we had finished.

Verley's bedroom was directly over the living room and I could see
a little pattern of light in the floor where an open grillwork let some heat
from below come up into the room. After Verley had gone immediately
to sleep I could hear voices. At last, Mr. Henderson was talking! I crept
out of bed and lay on the floor with my ear to the grating.

"Who's the girl?" he asked. Not the pretty little girl, or the smart
little girl, just, who's the girl?

I waited eagerly for the answer. Mrs. Henderson would surely say
something nice about me. "One of that Foster tribe who moved into the
McDonald place last summer."

Tribe! I cringed but kept on listening as Mrs Henderson went on.
"Don't reckon they'll stay long. Foster's sort of a drifter, they say."

"If he's leasin' from McDonald he'll likely get took," Mr.
Henderson said. "That guy is crooked as a dog's hind leg."

"Verley likes this little Nellie," Mrs. Henderson was speaking again.
"They're poor as Job's turkey but I guess it won't hurt none for them to
play together."

The light dimmed as Mr. Henderson turned out the lamp. "Let's
hit the hay, morning comes early." He yawned loudly.

I crawled back into bed, carefully keeping as far from obliviously
snoring Verley as possible. I was so sick to my stomach I thought I
might throw up but there wasn't any slop jar so I kept swallowing hard
and saying over and over to myself one of my brother Roger's favorite
expressions . . . "It's just a case of mind over matter . . . it's just a case
of mind over matter" until I fell asleep.

In the morning, Mrs. Henderson combed my hair and gave me a
beautiful new blue hair ribbon, heavy moire silk with silvery water marks
running through it.

"That color blue don't look good on Verley," she explained.

I stood on a chair to look into the mirror over the dresser in
Verley's room and thought how fine I looked, just like I belonged to a
rich family like the Henderson's.

Mr. Henderson drove us silently to school in the buggy and let us
out without saying goodbye. I saw my sisters coming into the
schoolyard at the same time. I walked slowly along with Verley, holding
my knitted hood by the strings in one hand so as to show the
resplendent hair ribbon.

Evelyn and Kate came over to me and asked. "Did you have a
good time? Tell us about it, Nellie."

"It was real nice," I said formally. "Verley's mother made cocoa
for breakfast and we had marshmallows in it."

Verley walked ahead and Kate said in a lower tone. "What were
they like? What did you do? Did Mrs. Henderson read aloud after
supper like Mama does? Was Mr. Henderson jolly?"

I talked without opening my mouth very wide. "They're real fine people. Mrs. Henderson gave me this ribbon and we played with Verley's boughten paper dolls. One has ten different dresses. And we had an egg for breakfast."

At noon I ate the lunch Mrs. Henderson had packed into my tin syrup bucket. There was a banana in it and I ate it all without sharing with my sisters.

A whole banana is not as good as you think it is going to be. It leaves a taste in your mouth like raw chalk.

Author note. *Betty Evenson was born in Kansas, but has spent most of her life in Wyoming. Her most widely published work is in the confession story field but she has also written features and short fiction for secondary slicks and religious publications. She is currently working on a nostalgic book about her memories of earlier days. In addition to Wyoming Writers, she is a member of Western Writers of America and the Wyoming Press Women.*

THE BASTARD
by
Margaret K. Look

It was the rush hour in Pittsburgh on a hot afternoon in August 1953. People were hurrying along the sidewalk, anxious to get home. At every corner there were crowds waiting to cross the street or to board streetcars. This was the day I met the bastard.

The heat seethed up from the pavement and out from the tall buildings, trapped in the concrete maze of the city. The traffic moving along the streets pushed the hot air aside, creating warm, unpleasant breezes.

A newsboy was hawking his papers at a newsstand. His red plaid shirt, wet with perspiration, stuck to his back. His sleeves were rolled up, revealing smudges on his arms. His hair was mousy brown, its ragged edges hanging over his ears and down to the nape of his neck. Tied around his waist was a small, black apron which had two pockets, one for coins and one for bills. He kept one of his hands in the pocket containing the coins, jiggling them as he walked back and forth in front of his stand. Under his other arm he carried several papers. "Read all about it!" he called, the words running together.

"Factory fire. Read all about it—just ten cents," he continued, his voice carrying down the block above the rumble of the cars, the honking horns and squealing brakes.

He walked back and forth, back and forth, turning his head each time he passed the stand to look at the coins scattered on top of a stack of papers. Another pile of papers had a brick on top to keep the papers in place.

I was waiting for a streetcar, standing in the shade of a tall building. A large woman, carrying a heavily laden shopping bag, stopped next to me and put down her burden. She wiped her face with a handkerchief and said, "Whew, it is hot. Every streetcar will be jammed."

I agreed, adding, "Nearly all the offices close at the same time. That's the problem."

"They should put on more cars this time of day, but they won't," she said.

The newsboy walked by. "Read all about it! Factory fire!" he called.

The big woman asked, "Do you know where the fire was?"

"On the north side of the city, I think. No one was hurt."

"I guess I can wait to read about it in my paper at home," she said.

A man in a gray seersucker suit hurrying along the sidewalk, slowed down enough to hand the boy a coin. The boy reached out with the arm that held the newspapers, took the coin, then gave the man a paper with the same hand—a skillful, one-armed maneuver that left his other hand free to jiggle the coins in his apron. He put the coin in his apron pocket and continued his pacing back and forth, calling, "Ten cents a copy—just ten cents. Read all about it."

Several people dropped dimes onto the pile of coins on the stand, yanked a paper from under the brick, and hurried on. No matter how far away the boy was when someone dropped a coin on the pile, he quickly went back and glanced at the money.

Across the street a man waved and called, "Paper, paper." The boy ran across, darting in front of one car and behind another. In a few moments he made his way back, running between the cars again.

While the boy was on the other side of the street, a short, fat man stopped at the stand. His light blue suit fit so tightly that his hands and neck seemed to be squeezed out of it. He reached in his pocket, took out a coin, put it on the pile, and took some change. He pulled a paper from the pile under the brick and walked on, glancing at the front page as he walked away.

Just then the newsboy returned to the stand. He looked at the coins, then ran after the fat man.

He grabbed the back of the man's coat, yelling, "No, you don't mister. Give me back that dime. Give me back the dime you took off me!"

Everyone looked at them. People along the curb turned around to look. Those hurrying along the sidewalk slowed down, walked around the pair, and then glanced back at them. A streetcar ground to a stop at the corner. A man, woman and two teen-agers left the curb to board it, all the time looking over their shoulders at the man and the boy.

The fat man's face was crimson. He was turned halfway toward the boy, who was yanking at his coat.

He said, "I didn't take your money. I put a quarter there and took only one dime and a nickel."

"You took two dimes and a nickel!" the boy shouted, still holding the edge of the man's coat.

A big, muscular man in rumpled work clothes, carrying a lunch box, stepped out from the line of people along the building. "Give the kid back his money!" he shouted.

The fat man tried to pull away from the boy.

The boy yelled again, "Give me back my dime!" Then he let go of the fat man's coat and shook his fist at him.

In spite of the heat I felt a chill going through my body. *This is a mob,* I thought, noticing that the people who had been on the curb had now formed almost a circle around the pair. I looked both ways along the block hoping to see a policeman, but none was in sight.

The large woman next to me moved forward and shook her finger at the fat man. "You'd take candy off a baby!" she yelled.

Then a young man in blue jeans pushed his head close to the fat man's and said, "What do you mean, stealing from a kid?"

The fat man pulled a handkerchief from the breast pocket of his coat and wiped his red face. "I didn't take your dime," he said to the boy.

He wiped his face again and then fumbled in his pants pocket. He pulled out a rumpled bill and thrust it at the boy. "Here, here. Take this dollar," he said.

The boy grabbed the bill and backed away, toward the newsstand. The fat man worked his way through the crowd, the back of his neck a bright red and his shoulders hunched forward as he disappeared in the crowd along the sidewalk.

The large woman returned to her place beside me. "That bastard! Just imagine, taking that poor kid's money!" she said.

People were again lined up along the curb and along the building, waiting for streetcars. And again the boy was hawking his papers. "Read all about it," he called.

I saw my streetcar coming and walked toward the curb near the newsstand.

A boy about the age of the newsboy came up to the stand and said to him, "How're you doin'?"

"Okay," the newsboy answered.

"Did you make anyone yet?"

"Sure did. Got a fat guy for a buck," the newsboy replied.

I turned my head to look at him, but he was already walking away, calling, "Read all about it!"

"The little bastard!" I said under my breath and stepped aboard my streetcar.

Author note. *Margaret K. Look is a native of Pittsburgh, Pennsylvania and a graduate of Cornell University. She was employed for eighteen years by the Post-Journal newspaper in Jamestown, NY—eight years of that time as news editor. She retired in 1977. Since moving to Wyoming she has lived in Powell and worked for the Powell Tribune. She has published articles and fiction.*

DEAD RECKONING
by
Charlotte M. Babcock

The hurricane season, like a massive prehistoric bird searching for prey, was approaching and the island seemed to tremble with apprehension as it shimmered in the tropical sun. The heat had become an oppressive force, dreadful and deathlike during the dark of the nights, while the days dragged endlessly, waiting.

Antonio Ruiz, head lifeguard at the beach of San Rios, felt the oppression and death was his companion. He could not fathom whether it was altogether the fault of the weather or whether the oppression was entirely within himself, but he did know that the death of his father lay heavy upon him, and he knew that this day would be very different from all the others.

Though it was not yet 8:00 in the morning, Antonio noticed the blossoms of the hibiscus and the oleander drooping as his bare black feet slapped along the asphalt promenade bordered by the heavy shrubbery. Their fragrance would soon become overpowering and cloying the heat. Antonio, who had always luxuriated in this tropical *Eden*, suddenly felt trapped and his dark eyes darted about involuntarily in a futile effort to find escape from the thick, reaching greenery.

Glancing upward, Antonio noticed the tops of the coconut palms swaying slightly. He longed to be up there, high and free as the morning doves. He shivered and his bare skin with its faint sheen of perspiration gleamed in the shadows like a length of black satin.

The beach, with its brilliant white sand, lay just to the right beyond the buffer of the shrubbery and the turquoise water of the Caribbean which Antonio glimpsed through the bushes glistened as it glided smoothly and softly onto the white beach, placid and beckoning.

Hurrying now, Antonio moved along the familiar walk, rounded a slight curve, and turned unerringly into a short break in the hedge where a wide, tall gate with a large rusted padlock and chain barred his way. He fished in the pocket of his worn, faded jeans and produced a key which he fitted into the slot of the big padlock. He opened the padlock and pulled the chain through with a grating rasp, swung the big gate back to the fence, chained it there, and walked onto the beach. He tested the sand with his bare foot and found it still relatively cool.

It won't be long, he thought, *until the sand will be as hot as the sun itself.* There would be a lot of people on the beach today. The heat would bring them . . . the unrelenting heat. Old Mother Luisa had said his father would die if the heat kept up and she was right, as always.

Antonio walked along the beach to the thatched hut where the beach lounges were stored, fished in his jeans again for the key that would unlock the ramshackle plank door and pushed it aside. As head lifeguard, all keys were his responsibility, even though he realized this locked door was so flimsy that it posed no threat at all to any determined thief. A couple of well placed kicks would demolish the door and probably the whole hut.

Antonio began dragging the lounges across the short distance from the hut to the nearest palms with a good deal less zest than he usually approached his job. He felt bad, really bad. In all the six years that he had been lifeguard on Oro Beach, he had never felt any worse about his job or his position in life.

Ordinarily a happy and carefree person, he was confused and frightened by this malady that engulfed him—this sickness in his heart. He did not know what to do about it. Never before had he felt the burden of his 26 years and his simple life—not like this.

It was almost too much too bear—the knowledge that all of his eleven brothers and sisters would bury his father today, all of them except him.

He, who made $40.00 a month, more than any of the brothers and sisters put together—he, who had the only regular job of any of them—he could not attend or participate in his father's burial. He prayed the spirit of his father would forgive him.

If he defied authority and went to the burial anyway, he would be summarily dismissed and someone—anyone—would be brought in from the street and hired to take his place for $30.00 a month. With the hundreds of unemployed street people in San Rios, it would be a simple matter—"no trouble at all," as the arrogant Commissioner of Beaches had assured him brusquely yesterday afternoon.

What could I do? Antonio worried, straightening out a yellow lounge under the dwarf palm.

He thought of the things that had never seemed so important before. *I cannot write well . . . I can figure only a little . . . I cannot show a school certificate in order to work in the government offices or the post office. I cannot drive—even if I had a car to hire out as a taxi. I cannot go to the bauxite mill . . . they, too, would want to see my papers. I have to stay right here,* he thought, *or Juana and the boys will have no one to keep them.*

Antonio and Juana had been together for almost nine years and in that time she had borne him five sons. He loved her more now, he knew, than when they had first come together. He thought of her beautifully sleek, black body and her eyes which could see into the very depths of him. He thought of her soft voice and the husky laugh that sent such waves of desire through him. He thought of her faithfulness to him and the five boys and her ability to keep all of them well fed and decently clothed on the little he could provide them.

He and Juana had longed over the years to be legally married, but it seemed to be something that was forever beyond his financial ability to provide. They didn't talk about it much anymore and the possibility hovered dimly in their lives like the small sailing ship that he could glimpse, its sail just beginning to drop over the horizon far to the west.

"How are you this morning, Tonio?" The deep voice which broke into his uneasy reverie belonged to Jesus Santos, his assistant lifeguard.

Antonio shook his head. "It is not a good day, friend," he said.

Jesus nodded in sympathy. He knew of Antonio's sorrow. "When will you bury old father?" he inquired.

"I will not be there," said Antonio bitterly, moving off to the lifeguard station. He unzipped his jeans and stepped out of them to reveal his white swimming trunks with the blue lifeguard patch on the side.

"What has happened?" asked Jesus coming up beside him.

"The Commissioner would not allow me the afternoon to bury my father. He told me yesterday afternoon when I went to his office on my way home," explained Antonio.

"God of our fathers—the pig!" exploded Jesus. "Tell me. What did he say?"

Perhaps the Commissioner could not have refused me so easily, thought Antonio, *if I were fortunate enough to look and sound like Jesus.* Antonio admired and envied Jesus his tall, muscular good looks and his rich, mellow voice—altogether quite in contrast to Antonio who was shorter, thinner, and soft spoken.

The beach was beginning to fill up now and the sounds of the happy voices laughing and shouting filled Antonio with bitterness for his misfortune.

"I went to his office and the lady said I could not see him, but I said I must stay until I *could* see him as it was a matter of great importance.

"The lady became very irritated and said, 'Very well. Sit down.' So I did.

"She gave me many looks and finally went through his door. After awhile she came back and held the door and said, 'In here.'

"I got up and went through the door and the Commissioner said, 'Well, what is it?'

"I said, 'Sir, I have come to ask your permission to attend the burial of my father tomorrow afternoon. I remember, sir, when you came to the beach before the elections and said that if ever there was anything you could do for me, I had only to ask. Therefore, I have come to you in my sorrow.'

"'I see,' the Commissioner said to me. But his eyes were flat and black upon me and I sensed that he could not see at all.

"'I do not think that you can be spared tomorrow,' he said. 'A cruise ship is arriving at our dock at noon and there will be many people on the beach. Because of that we would have to hire someone to take your place. If we must do that, he will be welcome to your job.

"'It would be an easy thing to replace you. You see my dilemma, do you not?

"'You would not like to be replaced, would you?'

"Do you not remember what—? I began to say.

"'I remember nothing!' the Commissioner interrupted me unkindly. 'I remember only the efforts which help me in my cause. Nothing else is important. What have you done for me that I should have cause to remember you?'

"I voted for you," I said boldly, although I trembled greatly inside.

"'I have important business waiting,' said the Commissioner, waving his fat hand at me. 'You must go now. The permission cannot be granted.' He pushed a button on his big desk and leaned back in his chair tapping his fingers together. His fingernails were very shiny. They looked like shiny pieces of glass on the ends of his fat fingers.

"The door opened and the lady stood there holding it open in silence and there was nothing else for me to do. As I walked by her I could not bring my eyes from the floor for fear that she would see my tears and sneer at me."

"The fat son of a pig!" exploded Jesus. "I would have smashed his face!"

"Perhaps. But you have no Juana and you have no little ones," said Antonio sorrowfully, bringing himself back to the present. "I could not. He frightened me."

"I am sorry, my friend," said Jesus, and his hand came to rest gently upon Antonio's shoulder.

They separated then, each to patrol his assigned area of the beach.

The day grew hotter.

Looking up, Antonio saw the sun approaching the meridian. He wished that today, of all days, he had something to eat for lunch. Ordinarily it did not bother him that he could not afford to eat lunch. But today it bothered him very much. It seemed more than ever to point out his lowly position in a world that had always before seemed better and brighter than it did today.

It will be a long time, he thought, *maybe even forever, that I will carry this humiliation in my heart.*

The afternoon wore on.

Antonio and Jesus were kept very busy patrolling the beach, for there were, indeed, many more people than usual who swam unheedingly through the safety buoys to get in the way of the speed boats or the sailing craft further out.

They had to pick up the empty lounges of those who left the beach. They had to bring out the lounges for those who came to the beach. They had to pick up the empty pop cans and the debris that could cause cut feet.

The sun beat down.

Suddenly, Antonio heard a shrill whistle. He looked up to see Jesus, silver whistle in his mouth, sprinting across the beach toward the water; where, some distance beyond the safety buoys, a bright blue sailboat had turned over. Five people—three of them children, as far as he could tell—were floundering in the water.

Antonio hurtled across the sand after Jesus and plunged into the warm turquoise water. Even though Jesus was a powerful man Antonio, with his wiry build, was a superb swimmer and arrived at the upended craft only a little behind Jesus.

He saw immediately that the three children were managing to stay afloat easily by dog-paddling. The man in the water seemed to be dazed and the blood pouring from a jagged gash on the side of his head was turning the water purple in an ever widening circle. The woman was screaming at them unintelligibly between choking mouthfuls of water as she tried to hold the man afloat, even though he was very heavy.

Antonio was shocked to see that the man was none other than the Commissioner of Beaches.

"The Commissioner!" he gasped to Jesus as they took hold of the sailboat to flip it upright.

"Madre de Dios!" panted Jesus as they swam quickly to the children and hauled them to the boat, instructing them to hold onto the sides.

"He is a wounded fish among the sharks," Jesus breathed to Antonio as they turned back to the man and the woman.

The woman had stopped screaming now, and as they neared her, she began an eerie moaning. Antonio felt chilled in the warm water.

The man had disappeared from her grasp and as Antonio and Jesus came up to her she snatched frantically at Jesus, babbling incoherently.

Eluding her grasp, Antonio dove beneath the surface and saw the fat Commissioner clearly some twenty yards below. A faint trail of purple, like a transparent chiffon scarf, floated from his head like the string from a balloon.

As he swam to him, Antonio could see that although the Commissioner was taking in water, there might still be time to save him if he were quick about it.

His mind seemed to weigh the chances with infinite patience. He became aware then that Jesus was beside him. Their eyes looked into each others' souls and they knew what they would not do.

Antonio gestured upward and they shot for the surface, breaking through for great gasps of air.

Antonio turned in the direction of the boat and saw that Jesus had gotten the children and the woman into the sailboat. The woman had not stopped her pitiful moaning and was holding fast to the children who were sobbing, "Padre! Padre!" over and over. At that moment Antonio realized with great clarity that he could not leave the fat Commissioner to the depths of the clear Caribbean.

He filled his lungs and plunged. Jesus followed him. They found the fat Commissioner of Beaches and, each one taking an arm, brought him from the sea.

The hearing to examine the causes of the boating accident and the tragic drowning of the Commissioner of Beaches was held at Government House and subsequently reported in the *Island Sun*, the newspaper of San Rios, side by side with report of the approach of the violent hurricane, Andrea.

The island community was saddened to read the account of the bereaved widow who testified that it was, unfortunately, due largely to his own carelessness in maneuvering the boat, that the late Commissioner met his doom.

Antonio Ruiz and Jesus Santos were commended for their bravery and unstinting efforts in the rescue of the family and the recovery of the body of the Commissioner. The reward, given by the Commissioner's widow and by the administration of the city of San Rios was generous.

Antonio took a portion of his reward to a monument maker where he was able to purchase a small stone cross for the grave of his father.

Soon after the cross was erected, Antonio visited the grave accompanied by his proud new wife, Juana, and their sons. As he gazed at the delicate, perfect cross, Antonio marveled that—with just one small act—the late, great Commissioner of Beaches had fulfilled his destiny.

He has been, after all, thought Antonio, *an angel of consolation to me in my sorrow,* and he prayed to be forgiven for the dark thoughts he had once harbored against the fat Commissioner of Beaches.

Author note. *A native of Casper, Wyoming, Charlotte M. Babcock has won many awards for her writing. As a graduate of Casper College, she received their Life Pass, awarded to her for excellence in Journalism. Her writing includes children's stories, poetry, fiction and nonfiction. Her poetry and fiction have appeared in Expression and her articles in the Wyoming Catholic Register. She is now working on a collection of short stories. She is treasurer of Wyoming Writers and received their Emmy Award for outstanding contributions to the organization.*

BE CAREFUL WHAT YOU WISH FOR
by
Margaret Hill

Almost the end of the school year and things haven't changed all that much. I am still a counselor at Ellen Cory High, and Rynn is still a student here. The difference is that Rynn cannot ever any more be simply my favorite counselee.

I'm not sure exactly when Rynn began to seem like someone special in my life. The day she first came to my office began like any other ordinary school day. Sleep a little longer than prudent. Dress carefully, but hastily, remembering the slate-blue eyeliner. Choose the multicolored peasant-style dress the kids like, and the stained glass earrings to match. Scald throat and stomach lining with coffee. Polish off a doughnut in four bites. Brush teeth. Rush out of apartment, remembering keys. Drive carefully, but as quickly as allowable, the three miles across town to school.

I entered my office to the familiar jangle of the telephone. The early morning caller was a Mr. McChesney demanding that I collar his son, Jim, haul him into my office and proceed to motivate him. I explained that my guidance skills don't include "collaring" kids, especially six-footers, and that I hadn't been successful in motivating my own brother when he was a teenager, so I doubted my ability to motivate someone else's son.

Replacing the telephone after the ensuing lengthy conversation, I felt bruised, not because of Mr. McChesney's demands, but because of that spot in the dialogue when I had wanted to say "my own children" instead of "my own brother." Again and again I find myself wishing to be a parent in order to identify with the students and *their* parents. But the continuing hurt is not just one of being childless. The digging pain is that of having been a parent and being one no longer.

That particular morning galloped along, beginning with a meeting of Whit Dietrick's parents, teachers and the school speech therapist to work out an appropriate curriculum for Whit.

After the Dietrick staffing, there was a visit from Frank Delaney's probation officer to check on grades and in-school performance. The remainder of the morning consisted of personal counseling sessions: parent-kid problems; peer problems; teacher-pupil conflicts; credit checks; educational and career planning.

Perhaps it was the beginning-of-the-day conversation with Mr. McChesney that left me feeling particularly sensitive for the rest of the day. In any case, when Rynn Cantrell came to the Guidance Office that afternoon to enroll as a new student, I sensed that there was something special about this girl. It wasn't only the way Rynn looked. There's nothing unusual about a slim waist, well-defined cheekbones, nutmeg sprinklings of freckles, or satiny hair the color of butterscotch. Rynn's attractiveness was a matter of warmth—the impression that she liked being at our school, that she liked being with me on that particular day.

So why should I wish one of the other two counselors would get back from lunch and register this girl? Was it because Rynn was sixteen, the same age my own daughter would be? But so were several hundred other girls in this school that same approximate age.

Sometimes I ask myself if I went into high school counseling in order to be around kids this age, or in order to have to face the reality of my loss. For whatever reason, I enjoy my job and can deal with the truth that I am no longer the mother of a baby I gave away when I was no older than my counselees are now.

During the process of registering the friendly, ebullient newcomer my bruises began to heal, and by the time Rynn had been introduced to a student council member who would help her get established, I was feeling good about the day.

Rynn came for counseling sessions on a fairly regular basis after that. When her transcript arrived from her former school, I called her in for a new-student followup. I lost track of the world for a moment when I noted that Rynn's birth date was the same as that of my daughter, Julie.

"Are you all right, Miss Gregory?" Rynn asked, looking anxious.

"Yes, fine," I said, coming quickly back from that long-ago moment when I, a child, had become the mother of another child.

"You looked kind of like you might faint," Rynn observed.

"It is a bit warm in here." I stood up and cranked the window open, relieved to have my back to Rynn for a comma's pause.

After that day Rynn and I visited about everyday matters—school work, band, FTA, boyfriends. It was only on the subject of parents that Rynn's words lagged. Mostly her ideas tumbled forth one upon another. A single question was an invitation for a bushel of teenage philosophy.

"How did you feel about leaving another school to come here?" I asked during one of our get-acquainted sessions.

"Well, at first it was like I was a tree being pulled up out of my yard," she said. "You see, I'd been in that school system for practically most of my school life and I just felt like I belonged there."

"And then?" I prompted.

"And then my dad got transferred here and I knew I didn't have a choice." She looked down at her blouse and began to pull at a loose thread on the cuff. "Sometimes you don't have choices," she said in a wisp of voice not really meant for me.

"Scissors?" I said, handing her a pair from my desk drawer.

"Oh yes, thanks." Rynn took the scissors and cut the loose thread. "Let's see, where was I?"

"About not having choices sometimes. You were about to say—?"

"Nothing really. Just that you can't always choose. Like your parents and things. Anyhow, what I started to say, when we came here I just figured this had to be a good school because the kids here like it, and if I'd been here all along, I'd like it, too, and I'd just as well pretend it's my school right from the start."

"That's beautiful!" I said.

Rynn leaned forward toward me. "Well, anyhow, it worked. Everyone has been so friendly."

"Rynn, you mentioned something about not being able to choose some things, such as parents. Do you want to talk about that?"

"I really ought to get back to study hall," Rynn said. Her glance darted about the room like a moth in search of a light. "That dumb algebra, you know."

"Sure. I understand. Here, let me write you a hall pass."

Probing for personal information is a technique I seldom use. I won't believe that being a counselor gives me license to wade around in other people's lives uninvited. Sometimes, though, I found myself trying to peer through the smudgy windows of Rynn's life. That birth date had lodged in a corner of my mind and set up a festering there.

What kind of work did her father do? Manager at J.C. Penney. Brothers or sisters? None. Where had she been born? In a little town nobody ever heard of. Somewhere near Denver, Rynn said. This information was followed by the darting-moth glances and change of subject to remind me that I had drilled against a nerve.

Perhaps if I involved Rynn in a group—people in groups sometimes spill over more comfortably than in a one-to-one counseling situation. Has something to do with discovering that feelings are for sharing.

At Ellen Cory High we counselors work with groups in the informality of the "beanbag room." Relaxing on a beanbag is a welcome departure from the formality of the classroom. Working with groups gives us counselors a chance to reach more students than we otherwise could. The students learn much from their peers about the art of living.

Not only might the group elicit additional information about Rynn, but she would be a useful member because of her own quality of being "all together."

Rynn liked the idea of being included in the Friday sessions of my fifth period group. It didn't bother her that Ginny was recently returned from the state correctional school for girls; that Veronica managed to be in trouble most of the time at home, at school and in the community; that Charles sat on his beanbag like a heap of shadow, refusing to utter a word or acknowledge a granule of feeling; that Jenny made lavish use of obscene and profane language. For Rynn it was enough that these particular beings were schoolmates—boys and girls searching for help and a sense of belonging. Rynn's favorite in the group were the two Craigs.

"It's amazing," Rynn confided to me one day, "how those two—Craig Bane and Craig Fitzgerald—take care of each other."

"So you've noticed that," I commented.

"They're so afraid each other will get into trouble. Like Craig Bane telling Craig Fitzgerald he'd better start going to classes. And Craig F. telling Craig B. he'd better stay away from the kegger if he's going to be driving his car."

As I had predicted, Rynn was good for the group. The others accepted her and paid attention to what she said.

"Have you really tried talking seriously with your dad about how you feel?" she asked Craig B. one day. "It honestly does work sometimes."

"Can you give us an example, Rynn?" I asked.

"Sometimes I have to remind my folks I'm not a little girl anymore. I tell them they can trust me because they have done a good job of raising me."

"It's different when it's your stepdad, though," Craig said.

"Not necessarily," Rynn told him. "What if you were adopted or something?"

And there was the moment I knew I had been moving toward and pushing away from me at the same time. I just sat there with a giant ball bearing in my stomach, while the argument wove in and out around me about how being adopted was different from being a stepchild. It was like when you come to the end of a story and think, "I should have known all along."

And some piece of me *had* known all along. Rynn was an adopted child. She had been vague about where she was born because she probably didn't know. She had been born on the same day as my daughter.

Now, of course, I must open all those terrifying doors leading backward—I, who am forever telling the students, "You can't go backward even a whisper in time."

During our next private session I said, "Rynn, sometimes I have to listen to what people don't say. Is there something with you and your parents that troubles you? Unfinished business of some sort?"

"I guess I'm glad you asked," Rynn said after a few minutes of plucking handfuls of angora off her sweater. "It's something I need to talk about. My parents are the greatest, but I keep wanting to know who I *really* belong to. *Belonged* to, that is."

"Is that what you meant the day you said something about not being able to choose your parents?"

Rynn nodded and plucked some more angora.

"But Rynn, kids don't get to choose their *own* parents, you know."

"That's true. But what I meant was, I'd like to choose to *have* my own parents, whoever they are."

"If you knew them, you might not want them," I said. Silently I added, You wouldn't have wanted that self-centered, conceited, noncaring hunk of masculinity who fathered you, then bugged out. Mr. Hit-and-Run.

"Maybe not. It's just that I'd like to take that gamble."

What I wanted was to take Rynn in my arms and say, "Maybe half of your wish can come true."

When Rynn was gone I stared at the apricot-colored wads of angora on the blue carpet and knew my life could never be the same again. I was no longer just me—Erin Gregory, counselor, moving contentedly from day to day, trying to make up my mind to marry that really marvelous guy in my life, Stuart Clay, before I settled in as a middle-aged career woman.

Now my days were all on tiptoe with excitement. At any moment my daughter might come to my office to make an appointment. "Something happened I have to tell you about," she would say breathlessly. "Do you have a free period sometime today?"

For you, I have the rest of my life free, I wanted to say.

In contrast to the eager days were the bleak pools of night when I must come face to face with only me.

"Solving problems is a matter of choices," I was always telling my counselees. "Usually you have two or more poor choices. If there were a good choice, you wouldn't have a problem."

My poor choices were that my life could go on just as it had before Rynn came, or I could carry on an investigation to establish that Rynn was, actually, my own daughter. Beyond that point, my mind refused to move.

While I was still ping-ponging back and forth between the initial choices, Rynn and I had a conversation which helped with the decision-making. She showed up on a Monday during third period, her usual effervescent self.

"Miss Gregory, I don't know what I'd do without you!"

"You managed for sixteen years." Half listening while Rynn talked on in her bubbly way, I allowed my thoughts to carry on their own monologue:

I would have been a good mother to you, Julie—Rynn. Why did I let those all-knowing adults in my life convince me that I wasn't adequate to care for you, that I would ruin your chances for a proper home and family? How could I have put you up for adoption after six months of cuddling you and thinking of you as mine?

At least I could be a good mother to Rynn now. But the adults, I had to admit, had been right. Six months with my baby were enough to convince me that a sixteen year old with no money, no job, no education, no husband, is not ready for the immense role of parenthood.

I suddenly realized that Rynn had stopped talking and was looking at me with concern. Hastily I punctured the silence with words: "Rynn, what you just said—about what you've gotten from our counseling sessions—I wasn't aware that was happening. Could you say it again?"

Rynn laughed. "The way I babble on, it's no wonder. What I mean is, you have helped me to realize that I have to deal with the world the way it is and not the way I wish it were."

"For instance?"

"Well, for instance I was on that kick about finding my real parents. Like on those TV shows, you know."

"And now?"

"And now I know my life is all right the way it is. My adoptive parents are neat, and when they bug me, they are just acting like parents. So why open a door to an unknown room?"

Why, indeed? So now my days were instantly as drab as powdered autumn leaves. And in the black pockets of every night I grieved for my almost-daughter.

Then something happened to make the situation less hurtful. Rynn came running into my office before school one morning to see if she had left her typing book there. "I'm in a rush," she explained on her way out. "Have to get this picture to the yearbook staff before the bell rings."

"A baby?" I asked, squinting at the wallet-sized picture.

"They're running the band members' baby pictures in the annual," she explained, giggling.

"I must say you have improved with age," I commented.

I closed my office door and sat down and tried to decide whether to be desolate or relieved. Rynn couldn't be my daughter after all. The baby in that picture was as bald as Kojak. My daughter, Julie, had been born with an abundance of sun-yellow hair. I remembered, too, that on that ash-colored day, six months later, when the social worker came to take my baby out of my life, Julie was wearing a plaid bow firmly nested on the coil of hair on top of her head.

I put a "Testing—Do not disturb" sign on the outside of my office door. Then I sat down and laid my head on my desk and wept a several-year's accumulation of tears. My once-and-forever good-by to my almost-daughter, Rynn.

Life the way it is instead of the way we wish it were, Rynn had said.

Now I must reapply my eye makeup and put on my reassuring counselor face. I must take the testing sign off the door. In a few hours Rynn would be here again with the group for its weekly session.

You are Rynn's counselor, not her mother, I kept reminding myself clear up until fifth period.

"Did you get your baby picture to the yearbook staff on time?" I asked Rynn when the group was settled in the beanbag room.

"Just barely. Under-the-wire Rynn, that's me! You know, I hope I didn't really look like that when I was a baby."

"What do you mean, really look like that?" Craig Fitzgerald asked. "It *was* you, wasn't it?"

Rynn giggled. "Not really. You see, we don't have any pictures of me when I was a tiny baby, because I wasn't adopted when I was first born. So I borrowed a baby picture from Mindy Nelson. No one will ever know the difference. All babies look alike anyway."

Threads of teenage laughter and wisps of conversation kept floating and floating around me in the little room.

No one will ever know the difference, I thought.

Author note. *Margaret Hill holds a B.A. in elementary education from the University of Northern Colorado and a M.Ed. in guidance from the University of Wyoming. A counselor at the Laramie high school, she retired in 1983. She has written seven novels for teen-agers, four Public Affairs pamphlets, and many articles, short stories, and poems. She now lives in Loveland, Colorado but continues as an active member of Wyoming Writers.*

WIND SYMPHONY
by
Helon Raines

The wilted fragrance of pine caressed the October air as Tres Bovey hurried with the crowd through the scattered dry leaves, which snapped and whispered, breaking and blowing here and there. The muted notes of a french horn blended with a violin tuning in the distance, and those sounds merged evenly into the hushed conversations, the occasional audible "hello," "good evening" of the people. Tres felt good, walking briskly with the crowd toward the lighted entrance of the high school auditorium. The weather was mild for opening night of the Symphony. A slight breeze, a crisp forty-five degrees were only a frosty promise, a slightly exhilarating anticipation of the coming winter, as the patrons in congenial quiet, anticipated the coming evening.

In front of Tres, as she approached the ticket window, were a young woman and a baby. The bright blue eyes of the child blinked sleepily but curiously from the peppermint pink blanket. The mother adeptly shifted the baby. At the same time she put her wallet into her purse and swung the purse over her shoulder. For a moment the strap caught a few strands of her fine brown hair, and Tres noticed the triple "A" monogram on the clasp of the purse. The woman brushed her hair aside and ushered forth, ticket in hand, toward the auditorium. Tres watched for a moment the back of her head and the baby's blue eyes disappear into the crowd.

Tres was thinking of her and of her baby when she said, "Only one." to the attendant who, observing her serious attitude and evidently attributing it to her companionless state, responded, "You sound unhappy," a boorish comment Tres thought, which she chose to ignore. She pointed instead to the heavy glass between them and mouthed, "I can't hear you," at the same time snapping her own purse closed and swinging it over her shoulder with just a little extra bravado.

Her mood from the walk was disrupted by the young woman, her baby and the ticket seller. But, nodding to a colleague and to two former students, Tres secured her program and a seat and regained her anticipation as she settled into the front row balcony. She had forgotten the earlier scene, and her mind flowed with the rhythms of the introductory Beethoven, when she heard a happy squeak, then a squeal in the hushed crowd below. Looking down, Tres saw the baby flailing her arms aimlessly, but exuberantly, toward her mother's face. Another squeak, and the mother moved the happy baby to her lap, so she was somewhat hidden from view. Some patrons shifted in their seats, glanced toward the couple, and then, as the baby fell silent again, they returned their attention to the closing of the movement. For a second longer Tres thought about the young woman, named "A" and wondered why she would bring the baby to the concert and why she would sit downstairs so close to the front. She should be upstairs where Tres was. "Perhaps she's just young," Tres thought. Her speculations were terminated by the appearance of the popular conductor and the featured pianist. Soon the orchestra and the pianist were moving together, creating music that rippled and whispered to the crowd, seducing the audience into their private and separate worlds. Tres felt happier as she moved into her own welcome solitude.

At intermission Tres maneuvered her way through the crowd to a back hallway close to the stage entrance and to an outside entrance. Here smoking was allowed. Often it was pleasant to find among the musicians congregated there a student or two who wanted to share a thought on the performance. Tonight though Tres was thinking of her own work, a story that was not going well, and she lounged and smoked somewhat hidden from the hallway by a battered and barren trophy case. But she found her thoughts returning to the young woman just at the time she heard a medley of soprano gurgles trilling over the mumbled exchanges and subdued movements of the musicians and the patrons. On the opposite side of the hallway were equally battered and barren bookcases; there, even more hidden because of the angle of the outside door, were the young woman and the baby. Both she and the baby, now snuggled in the crook of her arm, appeared to be listening intently to a blond heavily bearded young man. Tres recognized him as one of the lead violinists. She had noticed him at other performances because in his tux and with his heavy gold-rimmed glasses, he looked surprisingly well-groomed, handsome, even cerebral, in spite of the length of his hair and the fullness of his beard and mustache. His appearance was virile, but his manner was always subdued, as if his moments on stage were private and unobserved. Now he seemed agitated as he slapped his right hand into his left. Tres could not mistake what he said, for his words were as sharp and clear as the sound of the cymbals' concluding clash.

"Allison, don't bug me. I'm done. I'll send what money I can for April." The baby's squeals stopped short, and she flung a tiny fist into her mother's chest. The mother did not move or change expressions, however, and only as the young man turned and strode briskly away, his heels echoing metallically against the marble floor did she seem to realize he was gone. Then she raised an arm as if to stop him but slowly dropped her hand to the baby's blanket, which she arranged skillfully, still following the young man with her eyes. When she walked past Tres, Tres could see her eyes were the same blue as the baby's. A scent of vanilla and jasmine floated behind her.

Tres slowly finished her cigarette and walked into the cool clear evening to grind the cigarette stub into the asphalt. A cold breeze swished through the evergreens, and she pulled her trench coat around her tightly.

Resuming her seat in the balcony, Tres found her interest in the music competing with her interest in the woman and the child. Allison had taken the same seat in the front of the auditorium, where Tres now noted she was facing the violin section and probably could look directly at the bearded young man, who sat in the third chair from the front. Tres raised her opera glasses to observe him better. He seemed as removed and serene as ever, as his body swayed easily into the violin he caressed between his neck and shoulder as expertly and as intimately as the mother held the child against her own shoulder, the baby's head tucked into her neck. The music washed over the auditorium, and Tres rolled into Faure's "Siciliane." She was, however, pulled from the gratification of the music when she heard coming from what seemed far beyond her, a familiar soprano gurgle, happily calling back to the harpist's notes. She was torn between interest and agitation as she reluctantly turned her gaze once more to the baby, now quiet, but determinedly rubbing her eyes wildly with both fists and fighting to keep her bobbing head erect. The mother moved her once more to her lap and again a tiny trill echoed into the closing notes of the flute and harp duet.

Others in the auditorium visibly squirmed, as Tres did also. She couldn't help thinking of the years she'd stayed at home alone with her own babies. She'd rarely have had the nerve to take them any place, particularly not to a concert, she thought. But then she had grown up being taught to submerge her own interest to the interest and good will of other people. She knew that wasn't right either. Still she wished this young woman at least had come to sit in the balcony. But then she couldn't see, or be seen, by the bearded young man. She looked at him again through the glasses. His violin, held by one hand, rested on his left knee; the fingers of the right hand drummed nervously against the other knee. His eyes were tight, and his jaw thrust forward. He no longer looked cerebral.

Neither did the conductor, who turning to the audience, adjusted his slightly tight waist coat more tidily over his stomach, cleared his throat and announced, "Would the person with the baby, please take the child from the auditorium." Then he turned briskly, clicked his heels, as his raised baton announced the beginning of the final piece. Tres could feel a sigh run through the crowd, even finding its way into the noisier, more proletariate balcony, as everyone seemed mentally to applaud Mr. Goodstone's pronouncement.

Tres riveted her eyes to the third violinist. The man sat erect with closed eyes, a posture that suggested to her a rigid determination to find vindication, or perhaps escape, in the dismissal. She would not look at Allison, but she knew five minutes later when a last dying, but determined, soprano gurgle wilted into space, that she would be one of the few who would not witness the long walk down the aisle to the exit. Even Copeland couldn't compete, and the music seemed to slide away from the audience and disappear with the woman and the child into the frosty night.

Tres left soon after. She felt angry and confused. It had been like a collective banishment, and she didn't want to stay with the banishers. Even if Allison were inconsiderate, maybe just plain dumb, she had a right. Didn't she? Tres walked on through the busy leaves, dancing to their own wind symphony like brown elves, bobbing over the streets, across the dying grass and around the tree. Didn't she? No, maybe not. Maybe the baby took her rights. Tres stopped and lit another cigarette. Unladylike to smoke here, she thought, as she strolled on more briskly against the cold wind pushing through her light coat. Who cares if I smoke here she thought? But she knew someone would care, if she were seen. A middle-aged female college professor returning alone from the symphony, smoking a cigarette was not a good image, not the proper image. However, Tres kept on smoking until she reached her car and tossed the waterfall of red embers into the empty street.

Then she saw Allison again in her early model Datsun, just where the cigarette was quickly burning itself out in a bright red glow. Tres could not see her well, through the smudged glass of the car. She could see that her fine long hair fell across her face, and her head was turned away perhaps toward the baby. Tres hurried to get into her own late model car. She again felt like an intruder. And she'd had enough of this woman and her baby she didn't even know, at least enough for one evening. But Tres knew, as she pulled the car away from the curb, she knew that Allison was crying. And Tres also knew she felt like crying too.

Author note. *Helon Raines has published fiction, poetry, and criticism in literary magazines including THE DENVER QUARTERLY, THE MISSISSIPPI REVIEW, FRONTIERS and others. She is listed in POETS AND WRITERS and in WRITERS OF WYOMING. Since 1978 she has taught creative writing, composition and literature at Casper College. She holds the MA in English from the University of Mississippi and is currently working on a dissertation on Margaret Drabble for the Ph.D. in English at the University of Denver.*

CHRISTMAS WITH ALL THE TRIMMINGS
by
Nancy Curtis

I stomped the snow from my cowboy boots, wiped my sleeve under my nose and knocked on the schoolhouse door.

Twisting my old Stetson in my hands, I waited. Let Miss Roberts open the door. It's all the Christmas present I need.

The McDonald boy swung the door open. "What *you* want?" he asked in that cocky voice of his.

"I, ah, ..." I peered around him into the classroom hoping to see Miss Roberts.

"Yeah, you what?" he demanded.

"I brought a tree." I pointed at the pine I'd propped against the log wall.

The boy stepped out the door. He poked critically at the branches. "We already got one. A good one." He smirked in my direction. "My Uncle Scotty brought a cedar."

My face burned in the cold air. Durn Scotty McDonald. Always right there when it came to Melinda Roberts. Durn his pretty hide. I shoved my hand between the branches and grasped the trunk of the pine. "Well, okay, I'll just take this . . . ."

"Bobby," her voice called. "Bobby, don't just stand there with the door open. Ask whoever it is in." Her voice grew nearer. "Why, Mr. Swartzkoph, what a pleasant surprise."

Bobby McDonald giggled.

In the doorway stood Melinda Roberts. She was not only the prettiest woman in Pine Creek Valley but she was also the only single woman. Well, there was Easy Betty's fat daughter, but she hardly counts.

"Come in, Mr. Swartzkoph." Her voice rang as musical as a snowbird.

"No." I tugged my tree upright. "No. I was just going."

She touched my elbow. "You've brought a tree. How nice. We need some boughs around the windows. Come in and see. We've nearly finished decorating for the program and dance tonight." She guided my elbow to the door.

"Stay, Buckshot," I said to the dog at my heels. Buckshot looked hurt and went to wait beside my horse.

The room was criss-crossed with red and green paper chains. A huge cedar filled one corner. I tried not to look at it.

"Bobby, Tommy, break off some branches from the tree Mr. Swartzkoph brought and trim the windows," Miss Roberts directed.

While Bobnoxious and his friend dashed outside to pull branches from the perfectly shaped tree I'd tramped through the snow for a half hour to find, Miss Roberts pointed out each child's work.

"And this is Marybeth's drawing of the First Christmas." My niece, Marybeth, smiled shyly up at me as she and Elisabeth strung popcorn.

"Nice," I said. It was the same thing I'd said about Elisabeth's star and Tommy's sleigh but my brain seemed numb.

A wire was strung across the front of the room and sheets hung from it as makeshift curtains.

"Let me show you what's backstage." Melinda Roberts smiled and lifted her eyebrows. I wondered how anybody's eyes could be such a bright blue.

We stepped behind the sheets. She pointed to a lump covered with a quilt. "Not much to look at really." She lowered her voice to a whisper. "The bags of treats for the children are under there and this year they each have an orange inside."

I'd leaned forward to hear the secret. She smelled clean like paste and chalk. I glanced around. We were really alone. I took a deep breath and quickly whispered, "Will you go to the dance with me?"

Bobnoxious crashed through the curtains. "Uncle Scotty's here to get me."

"Bobby, please be more . . .," Miss Roberts began.

Scotty McDonald lifted the curtain and stood surveying the area. "Hello, Melinda." he said and smiled at Miss Roberts. "Swartzkoph." He nodded to me. "Did we interrupt something?"

The way he said it made me feel like I'd been caught stealing candy. I looked at my feet.

But Miss Roberts didn't seem bothered. "Not at all. I was just telling Mr. Swartzkoph about the surprise you bought in Cheyenne for the children and was about to tell him how you've volunteered to . . ."

"What surprise?" Bobby interrupted.

"Oh," she sucked in her breath, "I almost let it slip." She smiled in conspiracy. "Bobby, go tell the children that it's time to clean up. Then help the little ones with their wraps."

"Ah, Miss Roberts." Bobby stood firm.

"Go on, Bobby," Miss Roberts said.

Bobby stomped to the curtain, lifted it and disappeared. Soon his voice began giving orders to the children.

Miss Roberts lowered her voice. "As I was saying, Scotty's volunteered to be our Santa tonight."

A chuckle snorted from me before I could stop it. Scotty McDonald as Santa. That ought to be good.

Scotty looked nearly sheepish for a moment. Then he smiled a Prince Charming smile at Miss Roberts and said, "Glad to do anything I can to help you out, Melinda."

I was still grinning when Miss Roberts looked at me and asked, "You were saying something when Bobby came in?"

The grin dropped from my face. Reality sank in. Scotty McDonald had done me in. Cedar tree, oranges and Santa. It was clear Scotty had things sewed up when it came to Melinda Roberts.

"Nothing much, I guess," I mumbled and parted the curtains. "Better be going," I said and headed to the door.

Miss Roberts walked me to the door and Scotty followed along. I could feel him towering over me. He was at least six inches taller and his nose was straight.

"You do some trapping, don't you?" she asked.

"Some," I said, wondering where the question was leading.

"Well," she glanced over her shoulder at the children and lowered her voice again, "the Santa suit is a little, frankly, moth-eaten and I was thinking a little rabbit fur for trim might be a help."

I nodded. I used rabbit as coyote bait and tanned the rabbit furs for my sister-in-law, Marie, to use to line mittens and slippers.

"If you could come a little early to the program and bring some rabbit fur, I'd have time to baste it on before Scotty needs the suit."

"Sure." I said and opened the door. "Marie has to bring Marybeth early. I'll send it with them." I saw a puzzled look in Miss Robert's eyes before I turned and walked out the door.

"Good-bye, Mr. Swartzkoph," she called.

As I swung up on my horse, Scotty and Bobnoxious came out the door. Buckshot ran to greet them.

"Still got that ugly dog?" Scotty asked and pushed at Buckshot with his boot. Buckshot stood back and a low growl came from his thoat.

He could see that I still owned Buckshot. He was only looking for ways to aggravate me. "He's a darn good coyote dog. He can sniff one out a mile away," I said in Buckshot's defense.

"You and your brother Ben still sticking on those little homesteads over east?" he asked in a way meant to belittle me.

"Yep." I was in no mood for small talk. "Come on, Buckshot," I slapped my leg and pulled my horse around.

When I rode up to the school that evening I could see Melinda Roberts through the window. She was welcoming parents and guests. It looked like a good crowd by the number of wagons and horses. This and Brown's Christmas party were the social events of the season in Pine Valley. I didn't really want to be here but Marie had said that Marybeth would be disappointed if I didn't at least make an appearance.

I tied my horse. "Stay, Buckshot," I said to the dog and headed to the building.

Miss Roberts shook hands with the Royces and then turned to me. She extended her hand and I shook it. When I started to pull my hand back she still had a gentle grip on it. She placed her other hand on top of mine and, holding my hand between hers, she drew me in a step. "I'm glad you're here, John."

She was beautiful. Scotty McDonald was one lucky fellow. As I found a seat beside Marie and Ben, my hand tingled. John. She had called me by my given name.

The program was fine. Singing, poems, the nativity scene. Scotty sat by Miss Roberts. About halfway through the program, Miss Roberts took a big white flour sack from under the bench and handed it to Scotty. He winked at Miss Roberts and slipped to the back and out the door.

I watched him leave, grinned and winked at his back.

"Up on the rooftop, click, click, click. Down through the chimney with old St. Nick." The children's eyes danced as they sang. Traditionally at Pine Valley School this song was the signal to Santa that the program was over and it was time for him to enter and distribute the treats which had been cached in a wagon near the door.

"Ho, ho, ho! Who wouldn't go?" They sang louder with each chorus. They began to stand on tiptoe and look toward the back door.

It started with one dog barking and growling outside. Soon it sounded like an all-out dog fight. Ben and a couple of men hurried outside. The singing died down as the children wondered at the noises and excitement. Miss Roberts's voice led strongly for a moment and soon the children sang with gusto again.

I sat on the bench and smiled to myself.

Ben came in and whispered with Miss Roberts. Her eyes widened and she went to the front of the room.

"Children," she called for attention. The singing quieted. "Santa just stopped by. He has many stops to make tonight so he left the treats and asked some of your fathers to help hand them out. He wanted you to know he'd be at Brown's Christmas party next Tuesday to meet you in person. And since he wasn't able to come in tonight, he left something special in your bags."

Mr. Brown and Mr. Royce came down the aisle carrying the box of sacked treats between them. The children oohed and ahhed and jumped. They hurried to get in line for the treats. Bobnoxious shoved two smaller children out of line and shouldered into the empty spot.

Miss Roberts, Mrs. Brown, and Ben were talking in one corner. I went and stood by Ben.

"I hope that wasn't too big a surprise, Mrs. Brown," Miss Roberts was explaining. "I didn't want the children to think that Santa wouldn't see them at all."

"I'm sure that we can arrange for a Santa by Tuesday but what happened outside anyway?" Mrs. Brown asked.

Ben shook his head. "I don't really know. I got there in time to see Scotty riding off in the Santa suit with a bunch of dogs chasing after him. Bits of fur and red flannel were everywhere. John's dog, Buckshot, came up to me and he still had a piece of fur in his mouth. Looked like coyote fur."

Melinda Roberts looked serious. She shook her head and stared vacantly across the room. Then she looked at me with a twinkle in her eye. I grinned and she began to laugh. I tried to hold my laughter in but it ripped out. Ben and Mrs. Brown looked dubious for a minute but it was contagious. Soon all four of us were laughing so hard that the red and green paper chains began to shake.

Finally Melinda put her hand on her side, took a deep breath and said, "You are staying for the dance, aren't you, John?"

While my mouth was still open she took my arm and we started back toward the children.

"Merry Christmas, Melinda," I said.

Author note. *Nancy Curtis divides her time between writing, crafting stained glass, and being a wife and mother. She and her family live on a ranch near Glendo, Wyoming. She is a past president of Wyoming Writers, and a recipient of their Emmy Award for outstanding contributions to the organization.*

THE VAN
by
Sharon Brondos

Jesse Rivers cursed and struggled with the slippery plastic steering wheel. The heavy station wagon lurched and heaved from one side of the highway to the other. Jesse frantically pumped at the unresponsive brakes and roundly damned all Company mechanics.

The wheel spun in his sweaty hands, and he cried aloud in anger and fear as the unleashed car leapt completely out of his control. It crashed through the flimsy guard rail and plunged down a small embankment, coming to a dusty, steaming stop at the bottom of the barrow pit. The engine clunked and died. Small dirt clods clattered like dried rain on the shattered windshield. Dust settled in a cloudy shroud. The cooling engine clicked.

Jesse raised his head slowly from the padded dashboard. His skull felt like his brain had gone granade, and the bright desert sun streaming through the cracked windshield wasn't helping. He groaned and reached for the door handle with shaking fingers. He eased himself out of the wreck and surveyed the damage.

Despair took a seat in his skull alongside the headache. The station wagon was totaled, the hood crumpled, the engine disemboweled, the front tires splayed like a tired old lady's legs. And, of course, the shattered windshield. The burning Arizona sun made the cracks and lines in the glass shimmer scarlet, as if they were smeared with blood. Jesse rubbed his forehead with a trembling hand and walked to the rear of the car.

His computer repair equipment was tumbled, unboxed and broken. Delicate tools and gauges lay like shattered bones among the scattered styrofoam packaging. *Thousands of dollars worth of Company property*, he thought mournfully. I sure as hell hope they give it an expensive funeral. Jesse turned and trudged up the dusty embankment without a backward glance.

Reaching the narrow highway, he stared in both directions. Nothing but baked, beige country. He had managed to crash on the way to nowhere, coming from nowhere, in the middle of goddamn nowhere. Damn the Company policy of on-site service. Damn the salesmen and directors who didn't have to travel halfway to hell each time a Company computer blew its electronic cork. Jesse looked up and winced at the sun's glare.

Shit, he thought wearily. He rolled up his shirt sleeves and jerked off his tie. He tossed it behind him and started walking west. The sun and the headache played racquetball with his brain.

After about an hour, the effects of heat exhaustion and delayed shock began to weaken him. His vision blurred, cleared, and blurred again. Cold images of water appeared on the road just in front of his aching feet, only to disappear mockingly when he stepped into them. His headache had gone beyond pain. It was a devilish companion that jabbed at his mind every time he took a step. He began to talk to himself aloud.

"Jesse, ole buddy. You know you're gonna die right here in this god-forsaken nothingness." He laughed, the sound a dry rasp in his parched throat. "Fits, though, doesn't it, Jesse. From nothing to nothing. No wife, no kids. No friends who'll take time off work to cry for you. Maybe a machine or two that might have some grateful memories, but . . . ."

Despair, a heavy spider-web of self-pity, wove its way into his bruised brain. Work. That's all he'd ever done. All the good times he hadn't had, vacations he'd passed up, girls he hadn't pursued, all taunted him with the death-legacy of a workaholic. For all eternity, they seemed to tell him, you'll get to savor the memories of all the machines you repaired in your short journey through mortality. Dust puffed as his loafers sluffed through the dry earth.

He didn't see the van at first. The driver had to honk several times to get his attention. Then, all Jesse could do was turn his head and stare dumbly at the big silver vehicle that was pacing him like an obedient hound.

Jesse stopped. The windows of the van were smoked one way so that he couldn't see the driver or the interior. He had always associated flashy, decorated buses like this one with the Southwest's hippie element. But he raised a dusty, sweat-streaked hand and croaked a plea for help. *Saved was saved,* he thought. *And I don't much care if the devil himself is driving that thing.* The van stopped.

Jesse swayed, weakened further by a sudden rush of hope. Maybe this stinking dustbowl wouldn't be his grave after all. He heard the deep metallic rasp as the side door of the van slid open. Footsteps gritted on the highway.

"You certainly gave him a chase, Jesse Rivers."

The smooth feminine voice soaked into Jesse's boiling brain like a cooling breeze. His knees buckled, and he caught the front of the van to steady himself. The metal felt deliciously cold against his palms. He blinked rapidly, trying to clear his dimming vision, not believing the sight before his failing eyes.

No hippie chick reached out her hands to steady him. The woman looked as if she'd stepped directly from a fashion magazine. Long platinum hair, angel face with wide gray eyes, fantasy figure sheathed in a silky silver gown. Jesse smiled and fainted.

Cold. A cold so bitter it bit his skin awakened him. The world trembled slightly under his back and his groping hand touched cool satin smoothness. Jesse opened his eyes.

He stared up into the louvered maw of an air conditioning vent. The icy blast was aimed directly at his face. He blinked and turned his head to one side.

"Too cold for you?"

A pale, long-nailed hand reached in front of his face and shut off the vent. The gesture brought a silk sheathed knee near Jesse's nose, and he found himself staring up a soft well, sided by two slender thighs.

I did die, he thought, *and I've gone to Heaven.* The knee slid back to nestle chastely by its mate.

"You were so hot," explained the angel face, "that I guess I got a little enthusiastic trying to cool you off."

"'S all right," Jesse managed. He tore his gaze away from her soft gray eyes and examined his surroundings. He was obviously in the van that had stopped for him. The rumble of traveled roadway shuddered his body pleasantly, and the sound of rushing air hissed a background in his ears. Curtains were closed over the windows, keeping out the deadly glare of the desert sun, and the only light came from a gold, glowing overhead fixture shaped like a miniature chandelier. Jesse lay on a narrow bed at the rear of the vehicle, a bed covered with pale satin sheets and a silky, black furred blanket. Beneath the luxurious covering, he was naked.

"I hope you don't mind," the woman said. "You were in pretty bad shape. I undressed you and washed your body. I hope you don't mind," she repeated timidly.

"No, I don't," Jesse assured her, wondering how she could possibly think she could offend him. He felt his face and throat. He'd been shaved, and all the dryness of sunburn and thirst was gone. So was his headache. "How could I mind anything you did?" he added. "You people saved my life."

The woman's smile dimmed slightly. She sat back and folded her white hands on her silken lap. "I'm just happy we found you," she said. "You could have wandered forever out there."

Jesse raised a quizzical eyebrow and sat up experimentally. His brain felt cool and crystal clear. He stretched his arms and shoulders, noting with surprise that even his arthritic left elbow felt greasy and good. He glanced at the woman. She still looked uneasy. Jesse wondered who was driving. Husband, boyfriend? Surely, no guy in his right mind would leave her closeted off in the back of a van with a naked man. Jesse gave her a warm smile.

"I don't think I was going to be wandering any too far," he said. "I don't know when I've ever felt worse than I did just before you picked me up." He flexed his shoulders again. "And I don't know when I've felt better than I do now, thanks to you."

Her face relaxed into a smile, and she thanked him softly. She reached forward and smoothed the cover over his thigh. Jesse smothered an electric response to her touch.

You don't, he warned himself, go messing with the gorgeous Good Samaritan when you aren't sure who's in the driver's seat. He glanced nervously toward the front of the van. The atmosphere seemed dimmer up there, the golden glow of the little chandelier fading as it fell against the heavy gray curtains that separated the driver from the rest of the van. A soft laugh brought his attention back to the woman. Her hand still rested on his thigh.

"Don't worry," she said. "He told me to take care of you." Her words seemed laced with a tender attention to more than just his health.

Jesse swallowed, unsure whether to lean forward into her silky softness, or to inch back, avoiding what could be a very dangerous situation. They could be a couple of nuts setting him up for a ghastly fall.

"Who are you?" he asked. "You used my name when you came out of the van. That was before you could possibly have known . . . ."

The woman gazed at him silently, her eyes brimming. Jesse felt cold alarm shoot through him at the sight of her tears. He had a sudden terrible certainty that he didn't want to know who was driving the van.

He grabbed the satin sheet to his waist and attempted to stand, putting his hand to the carpeted wall to steady himself. "I want my clothes," he demanded loudly. "And I want out at the next town."

The woman folded her pale hands again. The tears had turned her eyes to silvery mirrors, and Jesse thought he could see himself reflected there. Angry, scared face, carved into a mask by cold fear. Black hair, combed back by nervous fingers. "I want to get out," he repeated in a shaking voice.

"Why?"

Two tears trailed crystal down the woman's pale cheeks. Jesse stared at her, hearing the tears more than the question. He stood for a moment longer gazing into the gray concern in her eyes. Then he sat heavily.

"I don't really know why," he admitted. "There's nobody out there who'd even consider shedding a tear for me." He gave her face a long, searching look. "Why did you?"

The woman shrugged, giving the gesture the grace of a dance movement. "I know what it's like to be lonely," she said. She held out a long white hand to him. "And I know what it's like to know that nobody really cares if you live or . . . die."

Jesse cleared his throat. He took her hand. "Are we . . . that is, am I . . .?"

She nodded. "My name's Dove," she said. "I'm a call girl. I was on my way to work a convention in Phoenix when my car turned over." She motioned with her hand toward the front of the van. "He picked me up first, and then explained about you." She smiled timidly. "He thought we might like to finish the trip together."

Jesse looked into her warm eyes for a long time. After he'd read all his answers there, and had given back the ones she asked, he tugged gently on her hand, and she came onto the bed with him in a soft gray swirly swarm of silk and hair and skin. From the front of the van came the sound of pleased laughter.

The sapphire and ruby flash of the highway patrol cruiser spotlighted the pale, blood-streaked face of the dead man. His eyes were closed, dark lashes lying on his cheeks like small, furred animals. A gentle smile turned his mouth just enough to press laugh lines into his thin cheeks.

"Never seen one looked this happy about it," muttered one of the patrolmen. He shoved his hat back and scratched at his sweaty, graying hair. "Except for all the blood, it don't hardly seem like he's dead."

A younger, slimmer cop was crouched on the passenger seat, rummaging through the glove compartment. "He's dead all right," he commented dryly. "Just lean in here and take a whiff. No telling how long he's been here. You did say the meat wagon was coming right out?"

The older man nodded and wiped sweat off his lined forehead with a soiled handkerchief. *Damn shame*, he thought, looking down at Jesse's corpse. *First the little hooker, smashed up in her convertible, and now this computer guy. Well*, he thought philosophically, waving his handkerchief at a fat fly investigating the congealed blood near the closed eye of the peaceful face, *when your time's up, you go.*

He fingered the blood-streaked crack in the windshield. At least they'd both bought it quick. This guy probably didn't even know it happened. He gave the body another glance before starting his slow way up the dusty embankment.

Sure would be nice, he thought as he trudged up the slope, *to know there was something out there that would give him that same kind of sappy-happy expression when his number was up.*

He grunted and pushed away the superstitious tremor the idea brought. He wiped his eyes and stared off in the distance down the road. Mirage water shimmered silver in the distance, and he could see the ambulance miles away, ghostly and indistinct.

He squinted and slid on his mirrored sunglasses. No, it wasn't the meat wagon. It was just one of those damn hippie vans. Big silver one. Coming right down the highway toward him.

Author note. Sharon Brondos lives in Casper, has been writing professionally for several years, and has had two non fiction pieces published in national magazines. She has completed one romance novel and is almost finished with another. She has completed and is actively marketing half a dozen short stories and an equal number of poems.

GATHER DOWN THE STARS
by
David Mouat

Summer darkness is a time for games on the northern prairies. When the sun leaves the sagebrush land, the sky glistens with winking, blinking stars and showers of meteors. Darkness is the time for hide-and-seek. Crickets chirp a song of constant alarm; bullfrogs croak seductively. A cloud passes over the moon, and everything is hidden and cannot be found. When the moon returns, bats swoop after whirring moths and owls sweep over the silvery, moonlit land and spot and pursue prey. This game is for keeps. There are only winners, never losers.

Jimmy Clark wishes it would not be dark. It is hot, late July, and the wind crackles through fields of ripened grain. Dust and chaff suspended in the air announce the death of season's work. Normally, Jimmy loves the nights, when insects bump-thump against the window screen and when the multifarious stars light the sky. He is thirteen, a boy.

Bo called an hour ago, said he and a couple of guys were coming over. Wondered what Jimmy was up to. Bo Balaschovsky, who slams Jimmy into his locker at school and raps Jimmy's head with his knuckles, said, "No matter about the past. I'll make it up to you, kid. You're on my team. Going to have a great time, visiting you and your friend."

"Me and *who*?" asked Jimmy.

"Just you," said Bo. "Me, myself, and I are coming."

"That means Kenny Watkins and Arnie Brown," said Jimmy.

"Yeah."

"Sure?"

"They're your friends."

"Yeah, sure?"

"Well, I'm bringing a surprise." And Bo hung up.

Cold sweat drips from under Jimmy's arms. Bo is no friend. The only friends Jimmy has are his books, thoughts, and nighttime sounds and sights. He understands their solitude but not teen-age jabber. At school, he stands aloof with hands pocketed. Listens. Mentally whittles away at absurd conversations. Imbeciles, they make no sense. But whenever he cuts in to clarify, he chokes and cannot speak. Moments of silence, the kids gawk at Jimmy, waiting. Laugh and whack each others' backs, while he strangles. Teen-age heehaws, Jimmy could never so intimidate another like that. Sometimes has tried but has lowered his hands limply to his sides and has shuffled away.

Mayria, who is visiting for the summer, and Jimmy's mom are snapping beans in the living room. They giggle. Mostly his mom, as if she were a girl. It is nice to hear her like that. Secretive, whispery. She has been this way since Mayria came in June. Daughter of a dear friend of the Clark's, Mayria has briefly changed his mother to laughter and smiles. And his father. Both are forty. Lately, there is no late night T.V. They are in bed by ten. They talk late into the night. Laugh, play, and plan.

Mayria says, "Come in, Jimmy, help. We're having a great time."

He does not answer. Pretends he's safe on his dark side of the moon.

His mom laughs, "Old party pooper."

Suddenly, Mayria invades his world. "Who called?"

He studies her features. Almost Indian in complexion—dark hair and eyes—she is beautiful. Her eyes are nearly Oriental. She wears a T-shirt, no bra: firm darts of brown strike his eyes, nearly blinding him. She also is thirteen.

"A guy," he mumbles.

"One of your friends?"

"Well . . . yeah."

"What did he want?"

"They're coming out."

"They?"

"Bo, Kenny, Arnie. I don't know why. They haven't come before."

She has made him talk when he does not want to. Laughter shines in her eyes, the questions are gone. He doesn't want her to leave. "Well, Bo said I was his best friend. He wants to visit. He's bringing something great."

"Oh."

"He didn't say what. Bo always has something new. It only lasts a week." Mean, rich Russian kid, Bo is, in Jimmy's mind. Even after all the bumps and bruises, Jimmy needs to tell her of him. He needs to share something of his with her, even if it is not his.

For awhile, neither say anything. Jimmy is nervous and tries to shrink from her. He wonders if she notices his skinny ribs. He scuffs his feet on the floor. Size eleven, flat feet. They call him "Frog Feet" at school, and he cannot even swim.

"Going to be a beautiful full moon," she says. It is nearly dark. The first crickets chirp, an owl hoots. The rim of the moon caresses the eastern hills. Pines haunt the blurred face of the moon.

"I wonder what the other side of the moon is like. This side's so close and warm." Mayria reaches as if to touch it through the open window. "He really is there!"

"What!?"

"God," she says.

For a moment, the world from which he is estranged is brought to close proximity, everything is clearly defined. He remembers slipping into her room and watching over her: shadows of leaves fluttering in the breeze shimmered over her. Jimmy had held his breath, bending so he could nearly touch the cones of her breasts which pressed against her nightgown. She had sighed in her sleep, brushed a bead of perspiration from the cleft of her lip, and slid her fingers across and over her breast and her stomach, finally resting between her thighs. She was golden and peaceful in her moonlit dreams, so eternally beautiful and close to him in the depths of sleep that he had wanted to kill her so that she could never be far away.

He says bitterly, "The moon averages 238,857 miles from earth; that is, center to center. During a lunar day, you would burn and at night freeze solid. Bring it to earth, float it in the Pacific. Then you could hold it."

She tosses her long, black hair. "Still, it's warm and romantic."

Of the moon's bright side, Jimmy is certain. Its volume is 0.02, density 0.60, mass 0.012. At most, 60% of its surface is visible. The rest is hidden, unknown to everyone but Jimmy. It has no emotional value.

Mayria grasps his hand. Warm, soft, the hand urges. "Come, let's snap beans. Afterwards, we'll walk. Talk about the moon. Whatever you want."

"Bo's coming."

"After he's gone."

She drags him to the living room. He stares at the sensuous arc of her hips. His does touch against one of hers!

—2—

Sparks meteor through the night. Kenny zings a rock across a rusty plow share. A bat dives after the stone Arnie hurls. Here comes Bo, spinning a dangerous circle in the gravel with his new motorcycle. Jimmy thinks Bo is going to smack right over him, but Bo cuts the throttle, hops off in a cloud of dust, snaps his goggles to his forehead, and socks Jimmy's shoulder.

"Like her, kid! Want to try her out? Hey, get your friend," says Bo.

They ring around Jimmy. Bo is a head taller than the rest. He has whiskers and has hair on his chest. Bo is barely foreteen. It seems to Jimmy that Bo has always been matured.

"I don't know." Jimmy is terrified of the machine, and he already wants them to go back to town.

Kenny rushes to start the bike, and Bo clouts him in the eye. Kenny kicks savagely at Bo. "Bastard," snarls Kenny, "you didn't have to do that. I was helping."

Arnie giggles. Jimmy looks like a last icicle clinging to an eave. "Shit," says Kenny, "have him get the girl. He can't ride it, we're wasting time."

Bo jabs Jimmy's shoulder. He winks at Kenny. "Start her up, kid." Jimmy stomps with a rubber, frog foot. Nothing happens. Kenny and Arnie hoot. Bo says, "Try again. Tromp it." Thumpity-thump, but nothing happens.

Bo steadies the bike, mashes the starter. The thunderous roar echoes through Jimmy's head. "Let off the gas," Bo yells. Jimmy's hand is smashed under Bo's mighty grip. The cycle is quieted. "Like this. Twist lightly." The machine purrs smoothly. "There, you've got the hang." Bo lets Jimmy manipulate the throttle.

Jimmy winds the throttle and jams the clutch. "Christ!" yells Arnie. "Wow." The cycle belches fire. Jimmy yanks at the handlebars to keep from falling, and the front tire rears high into the air. The bike pirouettes like a dancing stallion, then Jimmy is falling, and he dimly sees the cycle coming down on him. . .

From far away, "Jeez, I'm sorry, kid."

Arms are around Jimmy. Mayria's. She hugs tightly, and he hopes she will never let go. Soft fingertips trace his brows.

"God, are you all right?" It's his mother. She cannot touch him, is afraid he is dead.

Jimmy grins, nods. He feels kind of like a hero. *Blood and guts*, he thinks. Must have eaten a ton of gravel. It's good, all of them standing over him, worrying. He spits dirt. Probably, they think it's blood. Jimmy takes a calculated risk, and the words are magically there, "Damn, Bo, what a bike! Must have goosed her too much. Boy, does it have power."

Mayria laughs, "You should have seen yourself, Jimmy Clark."

Kenny and Bo stare at the girl. Arnie twitters. Jimmy's mother smiles and starts giggling, and everyone but Kenny is in uncontrollable laughter. Kenny is dangerous.

"Ride 'em cowboy," his mother whoops.

Jimmy continues his gambit. "Bo. Mind if I try again?"

Kenny surveys the girl. Jimmy's dad walks up, says, "Nobody's riding this cycle, tonight."

The moon is hidden behind the clouds. The stars are in hiding. It doesn't matter. Up there it is cold, down here he is in Mayria's arms, and is with friends. He laughs, jumps up, fires a rock through the beam of the yardlight at the stars. Jimmy walks over and pokes Bo's shoulder.

—3—

It was Bo's idea to play. Jimmy Clark is the best there is at hide-and-seek. Never caught, never "it," unless he draws the short straw at the beginning of a game. Then, nobody has ever made it to base without being caught. Jimmy is not aware of his prowess at this stupid group game.

Bo, Kenny, and Arnie hide together. Jimmy hides alone. Mayria drew the short straw. If she finds Arnie, he will be seeker the rest of the night. He is so dumb. Tromps around like an elephant, whistling. He is afraid of the dark.

Water drips from the tractor, a bat clicks after a moth, a mosquito draws blood from Jimmy's arm - Jimmy vaguely senses these things happening. Mayria disappears. The mosquito whines away. After a bit, Jimmy is not sure where Mayria is. She might be close to base, waiting for a run. She is good at this game.

He hides in a pile of railroad ties above Bo, Kenny, and Arnie. Arnie whispers, "I wonder where she is? Should we run for it?"

"Where's that little freak, Jimmy?" says Kenny.

"Hell if I care," says Bo.

"She's really something," whistles Kenny. Bo slugs him, but Kenny keeps right on. "Really something else. Did you see those knockers! Wish I'd fallen from your cycle. Umm, I can feel them in my ear."

"Aren't you glad we came? Aren't you glad I knew about her?" whispers Arnie.

"Yeah, big deal," says Bo. "If one of you guys would get caught, then we'd see."

"Not for you, not for anyone," says Kenny. "I have my own plans."

"Hey, let's run," says Arnie.

"Quiet," warns Bo.

It is too late. Mayria slips in on them and heads for base. "One, two, three on Bo, Kenny, and Arnie."

"Shit," growls Bo. "Why me first?"

Kenny snickers. "Now, she gets to hide with me. Too bad." Bo lunges for Kenny, misses, and rams headlong to the ground.

"Bastard, you're going to be seeker next game. You can bet on that."

Jimmy sneaked in behind Mayria, when she counted the others out. He is a foot from base and can hear her breathing. He reaches around the corner of the house, slaps the door, and hollers, "Free."

Everyone runs like hell when Bo counts. They expect him to cheat. Kenny and Mayria run hand in hand. Arnie tags behind. Jimmy slips to the top of the steel granary. He tries to think of a plan to get Mayria away from them.

When Bo is done counting, he kicks a dent in his cycle, then inspects it. Kenny has his arm around Mayria, who shakes it off. She giggles. Arnie tries to snake his arm in from the other side. Kenny stomps Arnie's toes. Atop the granary, Jimmy is more isolated than ever.

Suddenly, Bo gallops and knows exactly where to go. Kenny pushes Arnie into the light, and Mayria slips from Kenny's arm and vanishes. Bo ignores Arnie. He charges straight for Kenny, spies him, and whirls past Arnie, who is hopping to base on one leg. Just as Bo is ready to touch Kenny out, he falls in the gravel. "Free" Kenny laughs. Bo is up just in time to nab Arnie.

"Turd," Bo says to Kenny.

"Clumsy Bo can't stand up," heckles Kenny.

Jimmy sneaks in, says, "Free." Moments later, so does Mayria.

"Wow," Jimmy says, "how did you do that?"

"Same way you did," Mayria smiles.

"Hurry, start counting," Bo shouts.

Mayria whispers, "I want to hide with you, Jimmy."

Jimmy is surprised that she chooses to hide with him.

"Out of the way, Frog Feet." Bo flips Jimmy to the ground, and Kenny swipes Mayria's hand, and away they go. Bo follows, cussing.

Alone in the darkness of the railroad ties, Jimmy wishes Arnie would venture from the light. He wants them to go home, he wants Mayria to go to her own home. He needs to be alone, totally alone forever.

Kenny and Mayria laugh. Secretly. Jimmy tries not to watch but must.

Kenny holds her close. He rests his head against her bosom, but she shoves him away. Not too firmly, though. At once, he is back.

"What's wrong, don't you like me?" he asks.

"No, well, not that way."

Kenny tries to kiss her. She slaps him.

"To hell with you, then." Kenny mopes around, kicking rocks.

"Alle, alle, all's in free," whines Arnie, tracing the perimeters of darkness. He wanders aimlessly, knees together, head bent, knowing they won't come. "Come on, guys. Let's go. She's not worth it."

The night sounds drum angrily in his ears. The stars glare harshly down upon him. All is disturbed with him. Jimmy is alone.

Bo moans and rolls on the ground. Mayria hurries to his side to help. She holds him.

"I hear you guys," shouts Arnie.

Kenny is befuddled. Nobody has ever seen Bo cry.

"What is it?" asks Mayria.

"My knee, when I fell at base," whimpers Bo. He lets her roll up his trousers leg.

"That's a big gash," she says. "Maybe we should go in."

"Not yet," whines Bo, "I can't move. Just help me." She holds Bo, Bo holds her. She bends to roll down his pants leg. With a free hand, Bo motions Kenny. Kenny understands, Jimmy understands.

Mayria straightens. Bo crushes her in his powerful arms. Kisses her. Kenny falls on them, runs his hands over her hips, up and under her T-shirt, and onto her back. She cries but cannot scream. Bo kisses her long, hard. Then, Kenny kisses her and runs a hand down past her stomach. Bo gropes and grasps from the back. He yanks at her shirt, strokes her loins, caresses her ribs and up, up, straining to reach her breasts.

"Man!" cries Arnie, starting into the dark.

Ghostlike, Jimmy is down beside them. He swings a pole up, over, and across Bo's head. Misses Kenny, who hollers, "Touchdown!!" and runs. Jimmy smashes the pole across Bo's ribs. Bo is up, wobbly, limping to his cycle. Starts it and spins across the bridge. He and Kenny are going like hell. Arnie nearly keeps up on foot.

Mayria cries violently for awhile, then to herself, and walks to the house.

Jimmy hates her for leaving. He hates her for having promised to walk with him and to talk about the moon. What does she know about the moon!! He hates her for having been molested by Bo and Kenny. She has left him alone on his far side of the moon.

—4—

Mayria calls from the doorway. He does not answer. She will have to find him if she can. She calls again, then disappears into the darkness. He cannot tell where she might be.

He longs for his old friends, the distant planets and stars. He listens for the rhythm of cicada drumming from the trees. He has always felt a part of them, but now he is apart from them. He is infinitely lonely.

The dead, ripened grain cackles cruelly at him in the breeze.

His neck hairs bristle. Something warm reaches into his world. Mayria touches him.

She squeezes in tight next to him. He cannot avoid her nearness. She reaches for his hand, but he withdraws it.

For a long time they are still.

She says, "You saved me."

He wants to scream, he wants to shout that he wishes that he had let them violate her, as she had violated him, but he says nothing. It is the best way he knows to wound her.

She begins to cry.

At first, he is glad that in some way she has to compensate for what she has done to him. However, after several minutes, he recognizes the same hollow plea in her sobbing that he always feels.

He is shaken. He only knows of one thing to do. He searches for her hand, grasps it gently in his until he realizes it is the first generous gesture he has ever made. Then, he starts crying and squeezes her hand harder than he has ever squeezed a living thing.

They cry together, until neither need to any longer.

He grins to himself, when he realizes that for the first time someone found him and that for the first time he has reached out for someone else.

Her breath quickens, her pulse thumps.

She says, "I saw you the other night. You came to my bedroom. At first, I was frightened. But I trusted you and didn't mind."

He removes his hand from hers, tastes the salt from where her hand has been.

She says, "Later, I saw you in your room."

He starts, but after a minute he doesn't mind. There is only the warmth of her human nearness, and he gathers it closer to himself.

They sit in the black night, sharing each other. A cloud passes over. Out comes a star. The bullfrogs drum.

She whispers, "Bring them in, Jimmy."

"Whaaat?" He knows, but wants her to say it.

Her scent is stifling in the stilled air. "The stars," she says. "Bring them close. Make them ours."

For a moment, he traces above the reflections of the stars from her bituminous eyes.

Then he laughs, "By gosh, they already are."

Author note. *David Mouat lives in Worland, Wyoming. Currently, he sells seed corn from September through April. The remainder of his time is devoted to writing. Two novels are near completion.*

THE BLAISDELL CROSSING
by
Jean Mathisen

They buried me in an unmarked grave. I will grant that they did it neatly enough, much more neatly than my brothers, those dolts, ever did our customers. Still, it galls me, they—those people down there in their fancy restored historical town, tell visitors that boothill is nearly empty, that the graves have been moved. And I am here forgotten, while that woman, that high and mighty bitch they made a heroine of, has a statue in the State House—and she murdered the same as I—in a way, she murdered me.

We Blaisdells came out from Kansas, having to leave our "enterprise" there somewhat suddenly, due to the untimely death of my father. He tried to lay with me one time too many and I knifed him, with his own knife. Mother was not grieved since the Bible does not hold with incest and she was tired of his pawings herself. So on to new and greener pastures we went.

The yellow press overpraised that golden field of riches in that damned excuse for a gold rush down below on Currant Creek. But dreamers that my brothers, Rafe and Jeb were, it was here we came on the Pearson's Trace, a cut-off on that blasted trail to Oregon. Here at Currant Creek a hoard of fools had descended.

Mother and I, both much more practical than those idiots I called brothers, finally persuaded them to move down the canyon a few miles and set up a road ranch for weary travelers. And here we would feed them, I would bed them, and my brothers would give them their rest—a final one, so to speak.

We were selective of our clientele. Being a petite brunette with large imploring, blue-violet eyes (at least when I wanted them to be), we could usually pick and choose at will.

Mother was a miserable cook and a worse housekeeper; however, our travelers did not seem to mind much when my sweet young self was about to serve, flatter, flutter and flirt. Still, I had to keep cautioning Jeb about sharpening Pa's hunting knife during my act—for some reason it sometimes disturbed the gentlemen.

We had been doing business for some several months as I recall it now and had taken "care" of several customers in that time. Rafe usually disposed of the remains in the myriad of mine shafts that had been scattered over the hills by miners. Sometimes though, if another customer happened by too soon, Jeb would hastily plant our deceased visitors in the barnyard.

In late September on a particularly cold and frosty night a young man bumbled onto the ranch purely by mistake. Such a hayseed I have never seen and though he didn't have much with him, Rafe became intrigued with an old and worn ring the young gent—Joe Brayton, his name was—was wearing. I tried to tell Rafe that it was only a worthless gimcrack, but he swore he would have it and I had better get to my part of the show. Somehow, even to my cold heart, it seemed a shame to snuff out this particular young fellow. He reminded me of an awkward puppy. Then for some reason—I'm not sure if it was because Jeb was sharpening the knife again or what—young Joe decided somewhat hastily that he had sudden business at Currant Creek and just had to get on down the road. And he left before we barely blinked.

Since our business had been rather lucrative of late, we were not overly disappointed and Jeb had no great ambition to be disposing of bodies on this cold and frosty eve. And there we blundered.

Brayton did go on to Currant Creek and decided to imbibe a bit at the Elkhorn Saloon. In passing, he casually mentioned the Blaisdell place and how it seemed unusual that those folks were doing so well on what looked to him to be a seldom used stopover and a damned poor farm.

Generally, his comments would have passed unnoticed, but a latecomer to town, one Nathan Teague, an older gray-haired, craggy faced individual, did pay attention and he, too, wondered about our good fortune. Teague had come to Currant Creek not as a gold seeker, but in search of a young nephew, Billy McCall, whom he had raised. He had had a letter from Billy at the railhead, Bryan, stating he was coming on to Currant Creek about July 15th. Since then he had dropped from the face of the earth and Teague had come to find him.

And, as he pondered Billy's disappearance and the Blaisdell Crossing, he suddenly recalled vague tales of a stage stop in Kansas where folks had mysteriously disappeared and he began to wonder just where the Blaisdells had come here from.

The next morning the venerable Mr. Teague began to ask around town about the Blaisdells and found that little or nothing was known about us there. He also began to hear of a few other strange disappearances of certain wayfarers that had been routinely blamed on Indians, outlaws, weather, and the like.

After these findings, Nathan Teague decided the next place to investigate was our homey little way station. And when he came, he lucked out, for we happened to be gone at the time. Mother and I had gone to Currant Creek for a few supplies and Jeb and Rafe were off checking out prospective clients on the emigrant trail.

It seemed Mr. Teague proceeded to snoop around and his horse kept spooking near the barnyard, which was unusual because his gelding seldom spooked at anything. Teague was about to head back to town when he happened to see a glint of metal in the sage. When he examined it closer, it turned out to be a watch fob which resembled one he had given his nephew about a year before.

With fob in hand, he returned to Currant Creek and went to the Sheriff. Intrigued, the sheriff agreed to return with him to Blaisdell Crossing. At the time, we were all still absent on our various errands and Teague and Sheriff Ballantry began to forage around the barnyard and began to find some of Rafe's sloppily buried bodies; however, none were recognizable as Billy McCall, the nephew.

We were all returning home at the same time. Mother and I met Jeb and Rafe on the road on the rim above the ranch and all headed back together. At the edge of the rim I caught the glint of sun on metal on Teague's horse and then saw the two men who thought they were lying in wait for us. I called the others over and we quickly decided that northern Montana or southern Canada needed help from the Blaisdells and we'd better head that way rather quickly.

I underestimated Mr. Bulldog Teague and Mr. Bloodhound Ballantry—they trailed us for about two days.

We had camped that second night at Masterson Canyon, the edge of a mountain wilderness where it would be hard to catch us. Rafe and Jeb were feeling particularly cocky and had gone out to shoot a deer. They had just come back to camp when Teague and Ballantry caught up with us and began firing into the camp. Mother and Rafe were hit, but Jeb and I fired back. We soon ran out of bullets and Jeb was caught in the crossfire. Teague managed to sneak up behind me and soon had me bound. Before that dolt of a Jeb died, he confessed all we had done and laid most of the blame on me, including my killing of my father, the old bastard, back in Kansas.

After hastily planting my family in a rather shallow hole, they said I could take a moment to say good-bye and then we must be off. I said good-bye all right. I wished them well down there in Hell and promptly spat on the loosely slung mound. To say the least, I was damned perturbed that they had gone and died on me and left me to face the consequences.

So back we went to Currant Creek and they lodged me in their dark hole of a jail. To make matters worse, they used the front half of the jail as a school in the daytime and I had to put up with the twittering of those little jaybirds day in and day out. If I looked out the window I could watch the construction of my gallows—oh, what a cheerful world.

But they never hanged me. That, at least, I escaped. One night a rider went past the jail and fired into my cell with a shotgun and blew all my troubles away.

The irony of it was, we had not killed Teague's nephew. It was not until nearly 50 years later that the truth about Billy McCall came out.

That heroine of Currant Creek, Almira Haynes; she who nursed all the miners in the epidemic; she who was first woman mayor of the town and has her statue in the State House—dear Almira killed Billy McCall.

In a diary found in the attic of her cabin she told it all—how she killed Teague's nephew because he had spurned her advances and had then threatened to blackmail her because he knew of her gambling activities back East. Because she had become such an overblown legend in the meantime, the town fathers agreed to hush it all up and leave Almira with her statue while the Blaisdell Crossing was struck from memory.

Author note. *Jean A. Mathisen is a native of Wyoming and presently lives in Lander. She has a book of poetry and has had poetry published in several anthologies and regional publications. She has written several historical articles and short stories. She has been a member of Wyoming Writers since its start and was president of the organization in 1983-84.*

A SPECIAL INVITATION
by
Florence Burgess

George pulled the chain from his pocket and squinted at the gold watch. In a few minutes the big elm down on the main street would shade the Old Timers' bench. It was almost time to go.

First, though, he must put the final touches to his work of tidying the little house. Refolding the morning paper, snipping the dead leaves from the geranium plants, and changing the date page on his 1948 desk calendar took up a few more minutes. Then with another look at his watch, he left, closing the door carefully.

George was a familiar figure on the streets of the little town. With his walking stick providing a dependability that his legs no longer could, he picked his way along the path that led to the sidewalks. He was not at all unkempt in his appearance as older men often are, but rather nicely dressed in broadcloth shirt with tie. Neither was his face bewhiskered and serious, but clean shaven, with laugh wrinkles so deeply etched that he looked most of the time as though he were just slightly amused.

At the bridge that spanned the little creek he stopped and drew from his pocket a small sack containing seeds which he tossed to the geese on the water below. He loitered there for awhile, watching them dive and fight for the food he offered.

Turning away from them, he almost bumped into a woman crossing the bridge. Before he could apologize, she said, "Why, Mr. Bybee, you're looking so much better. Have you heard from Bob yet?"

"Not yet," he answered with his amusing expression more pronounced. "But I expect to any day now."

"Well, you surely ought to. Young people these days don't have enough respect. It's a shame."

Farther down the street a teen-aged boy pedaled his bicycle along beside George. "Have you heard from him yet?"

"Not yet," George repeated. "But I expect to any day now." Again he looked more amused than usual.

"Gee, I don't know why anybody wouldn't come for a great guy like you when you were so sick. I sure would have been here before this time."

"He'll come," George declared with emphasis.

The early afternoon sun was beating down on the little shops as George made his way past them to the Western Union office. There a young lady rose to greet him. "Hello, Mr. Bybee. How is my favorite customer today?"

"Well, I'm feeling pretty perky now. But as far as *he* knows, I'm still at death's door. What are you laughing at—don't you have any respect for your elders?" His voice trailed off as he, too, chuckled.

"Oh, I have respect for you, Mr. Bybee. I haven't heard anything, though. I've sent tracers and I have learned that the messages were delivered all right. He must have a heart of stone. After all of those times when he has wired you for money, and you always sent it—how could he?"

George was busily writing on a Western Union blank. "Well, we'll see if this will melt that heart of stone." He handed the message to her. "It wouldn't if I were on welfare, but as things are, it'll bring him out here."

She read aloud, "Funeral for George Bybee ten A.M. Thursday, July twenty-fifth."

When she stopped laughing, she continued, "When you start a project, you're thorough. You're also the liveliest corpse I've ever seen."

"Just keep me posted," George instructed gaily. Then, taking his walking stick, he ambled outside and around the corner where his cronies were already gathered on the Old Timers' bench.

"Is he coming?" one of them ventured.

"He will be here Wednesday," George reported to the assemblage. "He's expecting a funeral for me on Thursday."

Jeb's paunch shook with hilarious laughter. Around him the boys of yesteryear were boys again, enjoying this latest development in the episode.

Jeb wanted the full report. "Heard you went down to Frank's law office and changed your will. Cut him off, did you?"

For once George's expression was serious, almost sad. "Yes, I did. I didn't really want to since he's my only relative, but it didn't seem very orderly to leave my estate to him, even if he is my nephew. If he wouldn't take care of me, he wouldn't take care of my money—and I can't take it with me!"

Jeb was quick to notice George's pensiveness. "Well, we all wondered if you were going to leave everything to the ungrateful whelp. We know you've invited him out here time and time again. And we know that none of the telegrams we sent when you were so dreadfully sick got his attention. I say you did the right thing."

At the far end of the bench Clem was confiding to his nearest companion, "I heard in his new will his money goes for a refuge for waterfowls. That's a lot of bird feed!"

George's face had brightened. With his cane he rapped the bench for attention.

"The telegram doesn't say I'm dead. It just says there will be a funeral—and there will be—a big funeral party for all of us old timers. We'll start it off by singing *When The Saints Go Marching In*. We'll eat and drink and have a helluva good time."

Cheers and laughter rose from the group. Someone thought to ask, "What about your nephew? Will he be there?"

George's face again folded into the familiar laugh wrinkles. "Why don't all of you go with me to meet the train Wednesday? I have an idea that when Bob sees me, he'll look like a man who has just seen a ghost. My guess is that he'll get back on the train and leave town. But if he should decide to stay for the funeral, it's all right. After all, he does have a special invitation.

Author note. *Florence Burgess lives in Riverton, Wyoming and was an editor for Riverton's Family Stories in 1981. She has written historical articles for the Riverton Ranger and has had stories published in the Arts section of the Casper Star-Tribune. She is a member of Wind River Writers in addition to Wyoming Writers.*

DON'T INTERFERE WITH YOUR HORSE, AUNT MARTHA!
by
Gaydell M. Collier

Horses are taller now than they used to be. I noticed this just recently as I was trying to get on one.

It all came about last spring, when I found that I had accumulated some vacation time and had better take it before I lost it. You know how time creeps up on a body. When I thought about it at all, which wasn't often, I considered myself to be in fairly good shape. I'd watch myself in the mirror doing exercises and could usually pant to my reflection afterward, "Not bad, Martha! Breath's a little short, but really not bad!" I ate right except for special occasions, and slept well most of the time. All in all, I felt fit, even if my center of gravity did seem a little lower than it used to be.

But I was bored. In a rut. Maybe just a little afraid that life was passing me by, looking for a more lively companion.

"It's now or never, Martha," I told myself firmly. "You've got to wean yourself from the old guided tour habit. You need an adventure."

A few days later, I got a letter from my niece Sal. She and her family live on a Wyoming ranch tucked into the corner of a valley against the foothills. Sal's letter rambled on about Hugh and the kids, and mentioned in passing that they'd be busy with their spring cattle drive in a few weeks. It set me to thinking. I envisioned a picturesque scene with cows and horses, and me in a cowboy hat. A real change of pace.

I gave her a call that night. Two weeks later, I was sitting at the dinner table in front of a juicy steak, listening to Sal and the gang discuss the logistics of the upcoming drive. They would be moving a hundred or so cows from the home ranch to the upper place. Sounded like a lot to keep track of to me, and that didn't even count the calves and bulls.

"Think my Thunder is old enough to go on a fifteen-mile drive?" Soddie worried. His name was Charles, but they always called him Soddie—probably because he ate so much dirt when he was a baby. Now he was eleven, freckled and still grimy, and training his young quarter horse, Thunder, with help from his dad.

"Oh sure," Hugh said. He was tall and thin, with the rancher's pale forehead and weather-tanned jaw. "But he's still a youngster. Think you can handle him?" He winked at me.

"Handle Him! You better believe it!" Soddie was incensed. "What about Pete! Why don't you ask him that!"

Pete, the older boy, was beginning to acquire the long, lean look of his father. He had just bought a thoroughbred fresh from the race track. Rocket hadn't been winning enough, I guess, so he got canned. Pete sneered at his brother, shook back his rather wild mop of hair, and didn't bother to answer.

I got up my courage and asked, "Couldn't I help?"

Sal smiled at me. She could look like a fashion plate if she wanted to, but around home it was usually braids and jeans. "We hoped you'd suggest that, Aunt Martha. There's a real bad highway crossing and we hoped you'd drive up there and flag traffic for us."

Soddie said they even had a hot pink vest for me to wear, and then he convulsed into titters behind his hand.

"Oh," I said. "Actually, I was hoping I could ride."

"You, Aunt Martha?" Pete said. "You ride a horse?" The way he said it you'd think I'd suggested jumping a snowmobile over the Grand Canyon. They obviously needed a new image of ol' Aunt Martha.

"Of course, dear," I said sweetly. "Why, I used to ride all the time."

"When was that?" Soddie had a way of pinpointing things.

"Well, that was . . . hmmm." I hadn't realized it was quite so long ago.

Soddie nodded knowingly. "Riding was different when you were a kid, Aunt Martha. You probably wore a long skirt and sat sideways. Nowadays you're supposed to—"

"Don't be silly, Soddie," Sal said evenly. I imagined she was used to this kind of thing.

Pete said in kindly tones, "Honest, Aunt Martha, this is different. It's a long ride. You have to get in shape for it. Now that you're, uh, getting on—"

"Don't be silly," I said, catching on to Sal's nonchalance. "Trail rides are very popular nowadays. The ladies at the Koffee Klatch Home just had one and the youngest rider was 77." That may have been an exaggeration, but it wasn't too far off.

Hugh said, "Well, if you really want to, I suppose you could ride Cindy."

"Yeah," Soddie said. "She's getting older, too."

A few days later, as the sun broke over the horizon, I stood looking at Cindy who stood looking at me. She was a lovely golden color with thinning white mane and tail (I knew how she felt) and huge brown eyes.

"She's awfully tall," I said. Horses didn't used to be that size. They used to be short enough to get on easily.

Pete said she was the shortest, oldest horse they had. He took her over to stand in a ditch and I started climbing. "Also," Pete continued, "she's the smartest. Cindy knows cows inside out and backwards."

"Good for her," I said, grunting, and failed to catch the implications.

Pete pointed across the bench to where the foothills sloped together and rose steeply, lifting the highway suddenly out of the valley. "That's where we're going," he said. "That's where the bad crossing is." I barely noticed.

Soddie noted that the sun was getting higher.

"So am I," I assured him. "I'll have my leg over any second now."

There was a terrible racket going on—cows and calves bawling and an old bull revved up like a jammed foghorn. Dust steamed out of the melee, raising a pale, gold smokescreen that hovered in the morning sun, pungent with the aroma of trampled sagebrush. Hugh and Sal and the kids moved around hooting and whistling, urging the cattle out onto the bench. Cindy and I stood and watched. The whole outfit moved out, gradually developing a longish shape instead of an amorphous muddle.

"Let's go," I said encouragingly to Cindy.

She sighed.

We stood.

Sal came loping back on her chestnut mare, braids flying. "C'mon, Aunt Martha, give her a kick." She took off again after a confused calf that was going in the wrong direction.

"She's tired," I yelled after her.

"Don't be silly," Sal called back.

Cindy decided to walk. I grabbed the saddle horn. She was undulating a lot—maybe she was going to fall. She reached down to take a bite of new dandelion and one rein slipped right through my hand. I looked at it dragging way down there on the ground. Cindy lifted her head and turned around to bat her lashes at me. She practically put the rein in my hand.

I said, "Thank you." We were going to get along fine.

She finished the dandelion and walked on pretty steadily. I thought she was probably just waking up—needed a good cup of coffee. So did I. I began wondering about the saddle. It seemed very hard. Stirrups were on wrong, too—something about them was dislocating my knees. We walked and walked, but got no closer to the group.

Sal was coming back again. "Is everything all right, Aunt Martha? Give her a kick, okay?"

"Hate to," I said. "This saddle is very stiff and hard. It's probably hurting her."

"That one has the padded seat," Sal said. "and two blankets under it. Cindy's just taking advantage of you. C'mon, Cindy, hup, hup!"

Cindy began bouncing wildly. I hung on. "She's bucking!" I yelled.

Sal said it was a slow jog and I should relax. A crick popped up at the base of my neck, and I thought kidney damage might be permanent. Cindy walked again.

"You go on ahead," I said to Sal, panting. "Don't worry about us. We'll get along just fine."

"Okay," Sal said. "Take it easy."

I said I would.

Walked and walked. Dying of hunger. Been out for hours. I groped around in my saddle bag for the sandwich we'd packed before starting out. Ate it ravenously.

Hugh came back. "You okay?"

"Fine," I said, smiling so that he wouldn't notice my clamped jaws. "We almost there?"

"Haven't been out an hour yet," Hugh said. "Look over your shoulder."

The house was sitting right back there across the bench.

"That bad crossing is coming up," he said. "You'll probably catch up to us there. If not, just be careful and take it slow."

"I'm sure we will," I said. "How's your mare?" It seemed that this was her first big trip. She was fidgeting around, whinnying to the other horses as though she were afraid of being left behind. Cindy looked disgusted.

"Doing great," he said. "Just needs practice." He left rather fast.

Walked and walked. The second thoughts I'd been having about adventure and vacations were maturing nicely. They were almost developing into regrets. After all, I could have been soaking up sunshine on a Florida beach.

"Steel yourself, Martha!" I said to myself firmly. "Adventure cometh not by lying about. You are dashing forward to meet it!"

We kept plodding along, and I could see some milling around way up ahead. Cindy perked up her ears. The crossing was in a dangerous spot. There was a curve in the highway, and a junction with a gas station and saloon, and the hills rose up steeply on the far side. Felt guilty. Should be standing in highway in pink vest.

I wasn't sure what happened next because it was all pretty fast. I think a couple of motorcycles came around the corner at the same time as a Forest Service helicopter skimmed overhead and a logging truck backfired coming down the hill. At any rate, every cow and calf picked a different direction in which to run. Soddie's Thunder started bucking. Pete's ex-racehorse, Rocket, thought the starting shot had been fired and he was heading flat out at the edge of the highway, trying to pass the motorcycles. Hugh's inexperienced mare had gone to pieces, and Sal was dashing after a couple of calves. The old bull straddled the white line in the highway, chewing his cud and wondering what had got into everybody. They should have given him the pink vest.

Cindy, the cowhorse took in the whole thing at a glance. She was quicker than I was or I would have dismounted and left her to it. But we were off so fast I got wedged in—kind of a kneelock-hiplock-fingerlock arrangement.

We headed off a lone cow here and cut a bunch there. It was rather smooth, probably because it was so fast. Her head was low and the reins were streaming and I was still leaning back from the impact of takeoff with a death grip on the horn.

As we streaked along, we passed Soddie who was picking himself up off the ground. "That-a-way, Cindy!" he yelled. "Don't interfere with her, Aunt Martha!"

Not likely. Didn't know how.

We steamed past Hugh whose mare was planted foursquare, shaking like a jackhammer. I think he was holding his hat over his heart as he watched us go by.

"Yoicks!" I yelled reassuringly. No point in having him panic because of me—he'd be needed once all this was over. I wasn't worried, myself. My heart and stomach had jammed in my throat right to begin with, so it was only a matter of time before I'd keel over and perish. I'd had a pretty good life. As we wove and dashed, I almost enjoyed trying to guess what epitaph they'd put on my tombstone. "Died with her boots on" had a nice ring to it.

We crossed the highway, roared up a hill, ran back over onto the bench, charged back again. Next thing I knew, the cattle were all across the road, headed up the trail. Cindy stood with head hanging, her flanks heaving in and out. I sat with my eyes glassy, not sure if my flanks would ever heave again. Gradually my heart and stomach began descending toward their former locations.

Horses and riders straggled in.

"Great work, Aunt Martha," Sal said, grinning.

Soddie said sometimes I didn't seem so old after all.

Hugh asked how I felt.

"I feel very comfortable now," I said, "like I'm welded right to the saddle." Actually, I was beginning to feel pretty good. I had even resumed breathing.

Pete said I looked a little stiff. Numb even.

"That will wear off," I said. "I feel the joints loosening already." I tried stretching my facial muscles and managed a grin.

"Think you can make it the rest of the way?" Hugh asked cautiously.

I probably couldn't have gotten off if I'd wanted to, but why descend from my new found pinnacle? Thanks to Cindy, ol' Aunt Martha had achieved a new image. Even to myself. I was no longer a mere vacationer, I was now An Adventurer.

"Of course," I said stoutly, prying several fingers off the horn and patting Cindy's neck. "Don't be silly."

Author note. *Gaydell M. Collier and husband raise Morgans and Herefords on their Backpocket Ranch, twenty miles from Sundance, Wyoming. That is also the location of their Backpocket Ranch Bookshop. She has co-authored two books on horsemanship published by Doubleday. A third book is due to be published soon. Her nonfiction has been published in* **Smithsonian** *and* **National Wildlife**. *In addition to Wyoming Writers, she is a member of Western Writers of America.*

APOCALYPSE
by
Chris Hollingsworth

"Whew, what a nightmare!" the man said to himself. He was in total darkness. His body ached and was cramped, unwilling to leave its curled-up position. He felt disoriented and frightened. His voice sought the comforting presence of his wife:

"Nadine, are you awake? Nadine?"

He thought he heard a muffled response. It was probably much too early for her to be bothered. But he had to tell her anyway.

"This dream I just had . . . you know, that was really something! And so realistic! I guess that is the nature of nightmares, that they are so close to reality. But this was a little far-fetched. All the time while I was dreaming I thought this couldn't really happen, and yet, I was so scared . . .

I dreamed that I was in the den, mixing myself my usual martini before dinner. I had just closed all the windows and pulled the shades to block out the barking and carrying-on of the neighborhood dogs. I was looking forward to a quiet half hour, reading the evening paper with my drink, when the doorbell rang.

I went and opened the door, and would you believe it, there were four dogs standing on the stoop! I had to blink in the bright light—you know how the sun sets across our road—and wondered who of our neighbors would pull a prank like that, ringing the doorbell and running off, leaving those four brutes on our doorstep, when one of them started to talk! He said, quite mannerly:

"We are representing the neighborhood Canine Rights Organization. We are here on official business and would appreciate some of your time."

I must have been in shock, or maybe the martini had clouded my thinking, because instead of shooing the beasts off our property, I said:

"I guess I have a few minutes. I was just relaxing after work with the paper and a little cocktail. Why don't you come in and join me?"

Well, they came in—even wiped their feet, because there was a little mud from the afternoon shower—but they passed on the drink.

We went into the den and they introduced themselves. The big one, a white German Shepherd, was called King. Appropriately so, I thought, since he appeared to be the leader.

His next-in-command was a rust-colored Doberman, by name of Fang. I could have sworn he was the one that lives about four houses up the road; the one that makes our house shake every time he barks. He gave me a mean stare and pulled his lip back from his teeth just a little when he saw me studying him.

The third one was a Black Lab, called Black. He reminded me of the one we always see sitting in his tiny pen full of his crap, down the road a ways; the one we feel sorry for. He looked pretty peaceful, almost apologetic, and like he wasn't too comfortable about being with this group.

The fourth one was a little mix of a brownish color. He looked just like the little yapper that annoyed us so much last summer, chasing cars up and down the road for hours, getting the rest of the dogs all excited, too. His name was Rusty.

I asked them to make themselves comfortable and somehow expected them to lie down on the carpet; but they went for the chairs. Rusty sniffed around the cushions of one before he decided to sit on it; must have been the fact that it used to be Kitty's favorite chair when she still lived with us.

You know I don't usually have more than one martini before dinner, but I thought, what the hell! This is a highly unusual situation. So I made myself another one at the bar, while the dogs looked around the room and made polite comments on the furnishings.

King had taken my chair and looked almost as big as I, sitting in it with his legs crossed. Little Rusty tried to imitate him, but his legs were so short he couldn't keep them crossed.

"You may be aware," King started, stroking his head a few times with his paw, "that the dogs of this neighborhood have formed a protective organization. We have met daily for many weeks—sometimes our sessions ran well into the night—to discuss our growing dissatisfaction with our lives, especially where our relationship with humans is concerned."

So that's it, I thought. Now I know what the howling and carrying-on was all about that kept us from sleeping so often during the last few weeks.

"A few years ago," King continued, while Fang gave me a hard stare, "there were so few of us that we felt we didn't have much leverage. But fortunately our numbers have increased rapidly, and our latest poll shows that there are more of us in this neighborhood than of you."

At this revelation I couldn't help a little gasp, which earned me another reproving look from Fang. Rusty forgot trying to look dignified and bounced up and down on his chair a few times, yapping.

"In the past we had to handle our problems individually, with whatever limited means available. Usually we had little success," King said. Black nodded his head thoughtfully and gave me an encouraging look, like he wanted me to agree, too.

"We followed the activities of your 'Humane Society' with interest. They seem to have the right attitude, but are apparently hampered by lack of funds, lack of understanding or concern by the public, and so forth. Often they are nothing more than a—how do you say—a halfway house, or a prison. At worst they are executioners for many of us, whose only crime is having been born."

"I'm not unaware of the problems you people . . . uh, I mean, you . . . you all are facing," I put in. "But I'm not sure why you are here. Are you asking for my support? Money, something like that? You know, I do contribute to the Humane Society every year . . ."

Black nodded again, as if he knew. Rusty looked over to Fang for a clue, all a-quiver to give his support to whatever action he wanted to take. But Fang remained silent and kept his eyes on King.

"Actually, we are not here to ask for support, or to *ask* for anything," King said. "We have come to you as a—you might say— tribunal. You see, at our last session we decided to bring to trial all the humans in this area against whom we have grievances—all fair and square, to be sure. We will afford you all the rights and privileges under our newly adopted Canine Constitution and Bill of Rights. We have with us a list of charges, which Black will read to you in a moment. You have the right to address them or to remain silent, in which case you are automatically guilty. You have the right to legal counsel, and if you so desire, one of us will act as such."

I thought I hadn't heard right! Tribunal! List of charges! Canine Rights! I was willing to play their game as long as this crazy visit remained friendly. I have nothing against experiences on the fringes. But this had gone too far!

I put down my martini and said:

"I'm afraid time's up, gentlemen. Nice talking to you. But Happy Hour is over. So, if I may show you the door. . ."

Fang jumped up and leaned across the bar, glaring at me eyeball to eyeball, all his teeth showing, a low growl working its way up his throat.

Rusty leaped to the floor, yelping and bouncing three or four feet into the air, getting angry because he still couldn't make eye contact with me.

King said calmly: "Silence, please!" And to me:

"I will overlook your sarcasm this time. Please stand in front of the bar, place your hands behind you, no sudden moves. Black will now read the charges to you."

With Fang so close, I really had no choice but to obey.

Black unrolled a long scroll, stood up and started reading:

"We, the members of the Canine Rights Organization, accuse Mr. John Kernot of the following crimes against canine rights:

1. Chasing members off his property with rocks and abusive language, thereby interfering with their inalienable right to mark their territory and make deposits thereon."

"Hold it," I said, "you mean to tell me I have to let you guys use my lawn for your 'deposits?' Whose property is it anyway? You . . ."

"The defendant will not interrupt the reading of charges against him!" King snapped. "Black, please continue!"

"2. Harboring members of the feline family in his home," Black read.

"Hey," I said, forgetting the earlier warning, "it's nobody's business whom I 'harbor' in my home. Besides, Kitty has been missing for six months . . ."

"That is correct," Black whispered to King. "Remember, we took disciplinary action when she was trespassing one night?"

"Never mind," King said, "go on reading!"

"3. Complaining to our owners and occasionally to human authorities about members' barking, thus denying them their inalienable right to free expression.

4. Failing to show due respect and appreciation for our escort service by not slowing down when driving on public roads . . ."

There were two or three more 'charges', but I didn't pay attention anymore. My mind was still on their comment about 'disciplinary action' against Kitty.

"Before entering a plea," King asked now, "would you like one of us to represent you?"

"I don't even recognize these proceedings!" I shouted. "This is at best a vigilante action . . . totally illegal . . . a Kangaroo Court!"

"A somewhat inappropriate metaphor, wouldn't you say?" King asked mildly. "Since you apparently do not wish to have a court appointed lawyer—have you anything to say for yourself regarding the charges?"

"The hell with you and your 'charges!'" I shouted, even louder, worried about the fast pace of this 'trial.' "I want you out of my house immediately, and don't you dare come on my property again, or it will be a shotgun aimed at you instead of only rocks!"

"Add 'verbal threats and contemplation of assault' to the charges," King said to Black, and to me:

"You have not addressed yourself to the issues at hand. Obviously you have nothing constructive to say in your defense. Therefore I find you guilty on all charges. Sentencing will take place, according to our by-laws, as soon as we can assemble all of our members. Until then you will be placed into our custody . . ."

I was too horrified to offer any resistance. They surrounded me, and with Fang closely at my heels, they escorted me out into the backyard and shoved me into the toolshed. With all the gardening stuff in there, I had barely room to curl up in a corner on the floor. I was just getting real worried about the 'sentencing' when I woke up. Wasn't that the weirdest dream you ever heard, Nadine? . . . Nadine . . .?"

There was no answer, but he heard the sound of many feet, and growls and barking. He jumped up and hit his head on the low ceiling of the shed. He fell over a rake and was howling in pain, still on all fours, when the door opened and he was face to face with his executioners.

Author note. *Born in Bayreuth, Germany, Chris Hollingsworth graduated from Language and Interpreters' Institute in Munich, Germany. She immigrated to the United States in 1957, became a citizen in 1963, and has lived in Casper, Wyoming since 1974. Her fiction and poetry have appeared in Expression Magazine where her fiction has won two awards.*

BICYCLE SPILT FOR TWO
by
Bethene A. Larson

Before the meeting was adjourned, Paula stepped daintily over the feet of the seated club members, whispering "Excuse me, please." Tears of frustration threatened to spill from her large, dark eyes, but she held her head high as she stalked proudly from the room.

"Let's, er, uh, proceed with our plans for the Fourth of July race," Bugs Irwin, the bicycle club captain said, as I too, made my way past the subdued group. My hightop shoes clicked sharply on the hardwood floor; my long skirt fought with my short legs as I hurried to catch up with my friend.

I found Paula near the back door of the courthouse where the club's weekly meetings were held. She was tugging and yanking unnecessarily to release her bicycle from the newly constructed rack.

"Everything will turn out all right, Paula," I said, wishing for more adequate words of consolation. "They'll let you race with them—just give them time to adjust to the idea." Silence hung heavy in the cool evening air. "As you said a few minutes ago," I continued, "there are no rules that women can't compete in bicycle races."

"Oh, Grace," Paula said with exaggerated patience, "why do I have to fight for my right to be part of this so-called man's world?" She sighed heavily. "I get so tired of being accused of having emancipated female ideas—of being outspoken and ridiculous, and . ."

"They're concerned for your safety," I said, knowing full well as the words left my mouth that it was a placating statement, and probably untrue.

"My safety!" Her reaction was sudden and angry. "Concern for my safety—my left-hand eyebrow! They're afraid I'll win—and embarrass them."

"Well, you *were* rather threatening," I said, chuckling at the memory of Paula flinging her arms around like an evangelical preacher as she pointed out that Wyoming women were the first in the nation to vote, and the first to participate in state government—and that she intended to be the first to compete in a Wyoming bicycle race.

"My only threat is to their masculine egos." Paula retorted pithily. "Women *will* compete with men in sports—and not just tennis matches and croquet games! After all, this is 1892! There will be a lot of changes in our modern world in the next few years; you just wait and see." She paused to catch her breath and I hoped she wouldn't repeat her whole speech. "We don't live in the dark ages anymore. Bicycles have changed our lives—men and women both. Besides, if both men and women are welcome in the bicycle club, it's only fair that both men and women participate in all the events—not just the picnics and moonlight rides."

I strained my neck to look at Paula's face. She was five and a half feet tall, slim and beautiful. Her chestnut curls emerged from under her perky straw hat as she expounded her convictions, and the yellow ribbons danced emphatically with each toss of her head.

"Well," I said bravely, "the reason there aren't rules against women racing is because the men don't think we want to—and most of us don't." I was treading on dangerous territory now, so I raised my stature to my full five feet and courageously added, "I mean, none of the other women in the bicycle club want to race. Of course," I hurriedly added, "there is the possibility that some of the women in the Cheyenne club might want to race." I secretly doubted that anyone but Paula Reevers would be interested in being in competition with men, but the race was to be based on total minutes for cyclists—from the starting line to the finish. It was a cooperative effort that would prove which team excelled in the sport. Of course, there would be an award for the individual racer who finished first.

The two competing Wyoming towns had a long-standing rivalry, probably because of their common parent, the Union Pacific Railroad. During the development of the infant state, Cheyenne had been selected as the capitol of the state, while Laramie received land grants resulting in the location of the new university. And, although Laramie organized the first bicycle club in the state, within a year Cheyenne had thirty members in their newly-formed organization. On July fourth these two enthusiastic clubs would vie for their teams' honors on the prairie east of Laramie.

I didn't share Paula's enthusiasm for bicycle racing, but I did enjoy being a member of the club because of the social pleasures it offered, and because many of the members were my friends.

I had no desire for the stylish cycling clothes for women, referred to as "radicals", nor did I have an expensive bicycle. Paula had spent nearly a month's salary for her bike, and although I earned the same wages teaching at the same school, I couldn't justify spending nearly $40. The newest national craze might not last, even though the "safety" bike had been introduced for women. It was a model that had the bar removed between the seat and handlebars and had made the sport attractive to the women, although two-wheel cycling had been available to men since 1885.

My minister-father was shocked when I showed him my bicycle and told him I had joined the club, but when I mentioned several other women from our congregation who were also members, he calmed down. He did warn me, however, that many physicians were publishing warnings in newspapers that cycling was a strenuous sport for young women. I secretly hoped it was strenous enough to change my present image from "pleasingly plump" to "sensually svelte."

I labored to keep step with Paula, who wheeled her bicycle energetically on the dusty road leading towards home. The conversation lagged; each of us involved in our own thoughts, until I heard myself say, "I wish I could be as enthusiastic as you about the bike race, but Mama is depending on me to help with the Ladies Aid Ice Cream Social the afternoon of the Fourth—and anyway, I'm sure Papa would never allow me to . . ."

"I understand, Grace," she said in a resigned tone of voice. One disadvantage of being a PK, preacher's kid, is that people are quick to forgive us, whether we want forgiveness or not; not because of wrong-doing, but because we seem to them to be somewhat handicapped. I flinched inwardly as I recognized the familiar childish rebellion, although I was twenty-two years old.

I lived with my parents in the rectory, and would probably live out my life there, unless some acceptable gentleman rode up on his white horse, or bicycle, to rescue me. I was old-fashioned and traditional. I wanted a home, a husband, and children.

In all fairness, though, I believe Paula understood and accepted my stance. Liberation just wasn't my goal. Her life was much different from mine, and her attitudes more modern and progressive; probably because of her background.

Paula's mother had been a friend of Esther Morris, Wyoming's first woman to hold an elected office, and who had been influential in Wyoming politics the past twenty years as the state developed and grew. Mrs. Reevers, a politically aggressive woman, had often made trips to Cheyenne with Esther Morris, taking her young daughter with her. Unfortunately, when Paula was fourteen years old, her mother died, but the strong influence for women's rights continued to live on in Paula's crusades.

Professer Reevers, Paula's father, was involved with his university students and with the development of the curriculum at the new university, and so Paula's life had less supervision than most of her friends. Meals at the Reevers' residence were simple and unscheduled. Cleaning and laundry chores were done by a part-time hired girl.

As I dusted the Victorian furniture and washed the bric-a-brac at the rectory on Saturday mornings, I visualized Paula spending pleasant hours at the university library, reading law books (she hoped to someday become a lawyer) or writing in her journal (which would lead to the book she intended to write). And while I practiced the church organ in preparation for Sunday services, Paula sewed stylish garments to adorn her slender figure and dazzle her many admirers.

Reflecting on our friendship as we walked together, I thought how grateful I was that our lives had crossed. Our companionship had grown, not in spite of our differences in character and circumstances, but because we *were* different. Each of us gained a perspective that would otherwise have been absent.

"Yoo hoo!" A voice called from across the road. A shrill masculine whistle followed.

The two young men running toward us were easily identified, although the sun had sunk behind the western mountains. Cordell Meiers, tall and blondly handsome, and Will Chambers, shorter, but lithe and charming, approached us. Will's presence always caused my heart to flutter, although he seldom acknowledged me beyond a courteous greeting.

Paula gave the men only a silent nod. My own smile felt strained. I hoped my unruly blond hair hadn't escaped the hairpins in my chignon, but I restrained myself from checking.

"It's all settled," Cordell said, ignoring the chilly reception. "After you left the meeting we set the time for the race. It will begin at 3 o'clock. Twelve of us will make up Laramie's team—including you!"

"That was mighty generous of you to count me in," Paula said with an overly courteous attitude.

"Bugs will ask some local citizens to be judges, including some Cheyenne gentlemen too, of course, but we'll give a prize for the racer who finishes first."

"What's the prize?" she asked.

"Cash if a female rider wins, bicycling boots for a gentleman," he answered somewhat flustered.

Displaying his one-sided grin, Will added facetiously, "We can't lose—even if we don't win the race we'll have the best looking contestant, ha?"

Silence hung heavy.

"I must be going," I said, hoping Will would offer to walk me the half block to the rectory, but telling myself it didn't matter that he all but ignored me.

It mattered.

"I want to talk to the prof a few minutes," Cordell told Paula, "so I'll walk along with you. He was a graduate student in the math department under Mr. Reevers' tutelage, and was obviously in awe of both Paula and her father—for different reasons.

Cordell had come West the previous Fall from Cincinnati. Although

Paula thought he was very attractive, he was frustrated in his courtship. Had he asked my advice, I would have told him his frequent references to women having a high calling to be homemakers and mothers wasn't making points for him. Paula had told me that his attitudes were completely incompatible with hers.

Will Chambers, on the other hand, accepted Paula's female intelligence with compliments and encouragement. He listened intently to her views, at the same time entertained her with his sharp wit. Will was popular in Laramie society, never courting one girl too long for gossipers to assume he had serious intentions. I was not among those lucky girls who had the privilege of either accepting or rejecting his attentions, but I would have given a month's salary to accompany him to a traveling vaudeville show, or one of the seasonal balls.

I admitted to myself that Will was the primary reason I was a member of the local bicycle club, but I hadn't shared the thought with Paula.

"Will is always well-dressed," Paula told me once during a confidential chat, "because he gets his clothes at a discount at the haberdashery where he works." With pride, she added, "He'll be part owner of the shop someday." Oh, yes, Will had goals, in spite of his carefree attitude.

I saw little of Paula in the weeks preceding the Fourth of July bicycle race. She was busy designing and sewing her outfit: knickers of royal blue wool, a white blouse with a red ribbon at the collar, and a short fitted jacket with leg-of-mutton sleeves, lined and trimmed in red braid. Her white straw hat was decorated with red, white, and blue ribbons and she had purchased expensive white kid gloves to protect her hands.

The day before the race I stopped by the little house on Central Avenue and was directed to the carriage house at the back. I burst into laughter when I stepped through the door and beheld the scene. Paula was uncharacteristically dressed in an old cover-all apron, several sizes too big for her. She was diligently attacking her bicycle with soap suds and brush from a bucket, all the while chattering to the horse in the next stall who seemed puzzled with her confession of apprehension. With my greeting she switched the conversation my way and the horse concentrated on munching hay.

"I've been cycling four hours every day," Paula said relaxing as she realized the scene was amusing to an observer and joining my laughter. "I think I'm in good shape for the race, but I must admit I'm scared. What if I am the cause of our team losing the race? I mean, after all the fuss I made. . ."

I gave Paula a sisterly hug and wished her well, hoping her fears were unfounded, but admitting to myself the same apprehensions.

Due to Laramie's high altitude, summer days are usually cool. However, if the sky is clear the sun can send cruel penetrating rays toward the treeless plain. July 4, 1892 was such a day.

The *Boomerang* promoted the bicycle race as the highlight of the Independence Day celebration. The hot weather didn't deter the large crowd who gathered to watch the race. The wagon trail had been cleared for use as the race track and red flags waved gaily at the starting line.

Many Cheyenne bicycle club boosters boarded the Union Pacific train earlier in the day to travel the fifty miles to cheer their team. Local race enthusiasts had arrived with horses, wagons, and buggies, which were scattered about among the prairie growth. Mothers with shrill voices scolded children and dogs barked at the rodents that scurried beneath the sagebrush. An occasional exploding firecracker added to the confusion.

Papa agreed to accompany me to the race after Bugs Irwin asked him to be a judge; pointing out that the decision wouldn't be contested if a clergyman was present. Mama was agreeable too, saying there wouldn't be many people in town to buy the ice cream—they would all be at the race, although she didn't want to go with us.

As soon as we arrived at the site with our horse and buggy, I spotted the Laramie team. They were huddled together making last minute checks of their bicycle tires; seeming to have a good time, laughing and encouraging one another. Paula was in the midst of the racers, looking as stylish as an advertisement in the *Ladies Home Journal*, although she must have been uncomfortably warm. I was glad she decided against wearing her boned corset, though this was a secret between the two of us.

Cheyenne's contestants were uniformly attired in matching brown knickers, tailored checked jackets, and tight-fitting caps with an insignia identifying their club. Why hadn't our club thought of that?

A few of the young men from the Cheyenne team whistled at Paula and remarked about Laramie's suffragettes, but she ignored the barbs and appeared poised in the midst of the confusion. She was the only woman racer. Win or lose, I thought to myself, she *will* have that distinction.

"We'll drive on to the finish line," Papa said, urging old Nell to move into the growth of the prairie. "I can't judge the end of the race from the starting line."

I was reluctant to leave the exciting scene, but I waved to Paula and she raised a white-gloved hand in response.

It occurred to me the crowd of spectators would be cheering the racers by traveling alongside the bicycle route, off the trail, as we were doing in our buggy. It would be impossible to see the cyclists with the obstacles of vehicles, horses, and runners.

As soon as we reached the designated finish line, one of the officials explained the rules and gave Papa a large "official judge" badge. Papa withdrew his large Ingersol watch from his vest pocket and seated himself at his designated place. How incongruous he looked in his black suit and white clerical collar seated on a nail keg in the midst of the sagebrush.

A gunshot echoed across the mile long stretch of wasteland. The race had begun!

I couldn't see the racers through the cloud of dust and the heads and shoulders of eager spectators blocked my view. The tension was unbearable. I ran clumsily through the sagebrush, hiking my long serge skirt as high as decently possible, trying to get a glimpse of the racers.

I heard Papa call me, but I was determined to watch for Paula in her red, white, and blue costume—yes, and Will too. He should be easy to find since he wore a white cap.

The bicycle trail was much rougher near the finish line. Obviously the laborors who cleared the old wagon trail had become weary of chopping at the tough roots and removing large round rocks. It was an obstacle course that would take a skillful cyclist to maneuver.

Oh, Paula, I silently prayed, *be careful! Will, too. Oh, Lord, what are we doing out here in this wild prairie, racing these strange two-wheeled machines?* A deep fear, known to women through the ages, clutched at my breast and I was suddenly resentful of the foolishness that endangered those I loved.

Several cyclists passed by my side, when I saw Paula! She looked like patriotic bunting flying in the breeze. *Flying! Oh, dear God!* She *was* flying—and her bicycle too! The wheeled apparition crashed into a huge sagebrush, then Paula disappeared into the brush at the side of the trail, feet pointed toward the blue sky, arms flailing desperately.

My heart sank. I hopped, zigzagged, and ran, but before I could reach Paula, Will Chambers stopped abruptly, threw his bicycle aside and ran toward her.

But Paula was quickly on her feet. I couldn't believe my eyes! Disheveled and soiled, she screamed at him and pounded his chest with her fists.

Racers passed by, hardly noticing the drama as they pedaled frantically toward the finish line. Cordell passed by too, pumping hard, hunched low on his bicycle, his coattails flying.

At last I reached my friend, but I was inhibited by her strange behavior. "Paula, are you all right?" I asked breathlessly, wondering if she had lost her senses in the accident.

"Will should never have stopped!" she said, her voice pitched lower now as she pulled at the cactus thorns piercing her gloves. "I'm all right; just bruised, I think," she said shakily. "If there weren't so many people around I'd pull my knickers down and assess the damage."

"I'll turn my back, if that will help," Will said, obligingly.

"You've helped more than enough already," Paula said crossly. "Why did you stop? How do you expect us to win when you aren't in the race?"

Will was speechless. "Gosh, Paula—it was the only civilized thing to do," he said defensively. "I couldn't just let you lay out there in the sagebrush."

"Why couldn't you?"

"You could have been seriously hurt."

"You didn't stop to pick up the Cheyenne racers who crashed."

"They weren't women!" Will's voice was high-pitched now and his anger made him seem like a stranger. I would never have guessed he had a temper.

"I didn't ask for any favors."

"Well, I wanted to give them! For all I knew, you had broken your liberated neck!"

Paula looked at Will as if seeing him clearly for the first time. "I thought you, of all people, understood me."

As the boisterous discussion was taking place, racers passed by depositing layers of dust on us. Paula's cheeks were streaked with tears of pain and frustration. We seemed to be immobilized; the cheering for the winning team reaching our ears.

Paula rubbed her hips, brushed the dirt from her torn outfit and struggled for composure.

Will pulled his bicycle out of the brush, looking it over, and mumbled something about not being appreciated.

"I'll wheel your bike, Paula—you lean on me," I said. "It isn't far, and we'll go slow."

"She's not hurt," Will stated flatly. "She wouldn't have the strength to pound on me, verbally and physically, if she were."

"I'm all right, but I'm not sure my bicycle wasn't killed," Paula said glancing at her expensive bike as I untangled it from its landing place. The front wheel was bent, several spokes were broken, and sage and cactus debris clung to the dust-covered frame.

Paula remarked that she was glad she was well padded with her "radicals." Her hat sat askew on her head; the pins had miraculously held it on. I put my arm around her waist and the three of us made our way toward the celebrating crowd. The thought crossed my mind that we resembled the Spirit of '76—embattled, wounded, but undaunted.

Cordell ran to meet us. Taking the handlebars of the crippled bicycle he looked anxiously at Paula.

"Are you hurt?" Without waiting for her answer he began

apologizing. "I'm sorry I didn't stop, but the Cheyenne team was gaining on us. They lost four riders at the beginning of the race, and you seemed to be all right—I mean, on your feet, and I knew how important it was for us to win the race, and . . ."

"Oh, Cordell, you did exactly right!" Paula said as she flung her arms around his neck in an unprecedented display of affection. "I'm glad you finished the race."

"Ya, I wish I'd thought of that," Will stated glumly. "Paula really means it when she says she wants to be treated like one of the fellas."

"Whose team won?" I asked eagerly. The celebration gave little indication as to the identity of the winning team.

"Oh, we did!" Cordell said, realizing we hadn't heard the news. "I was so concerned about Paula that I nearly forgot." How handsome he was when he smiled at Paula. Their hands met.

"Well, then," Paula said with a twinkle in her eye as she gazed directly at her would-be rescuer, "you are forgiven, Will.'

Will seemed to be confused at her remark, so I quickly asked Cordell who the first place winner was.

"Bugs Irwin will win the individual prize, but our club placed first by seven seconds."

Will pushed his cap back at a jaunty angle and wiped the dirt and sweat from his brow. He looked down at me and his expression seemed to change visibly as he assumed his carefree attitude once more.

"How about you, Shorty?" he asked, apparently hoping to end the discussion about racing. "Do you forgive me too?"

"I have nothing to forgive," I said. "Some of us are just handicapped—but it's nothing we can help."

"Huh?"

"Never mind."

Will studied my face, as if seeing me for the first time. "By golly, Grace, you are a pretty girl. I wonder why I never noticed before."

"I'm sure I don't know," I said, embarrassed, flattered, and flustered.

I'm a winner too, I reflected, and I didn't even enter the race!

"Would you, Miss Grace Collins, be so kind as to accompany me to the band concert this evening on the courthouse lawn?"

"Indeed I would, Mr. Chambers."

NOTE: All characters are fictitious, however this story is based on an actual event which took place near Laramie, Wyoming in 1892.

Laramie organized the first bicycle club in the state, followed by Cheyenne the next year (1892), Rock Springs (1895), Rawlins and Evanston shortly after. (Wyoming State Archives and Historical Dept.)

According to *Bikereport* magazine, Missoula, MT., May/June 1983, "The bicycle was undoubtedly the major factor in changing Victorian manners and morals. It was a freedom machine for women, allowing them to escape the confines of home, permanently altering their dress styles, marking their first real opportunity to engage in an invigorating outdoor sport, and radically changing courtship patterns. The golden age of bicycling coincided with the tumultuous decade known ever since as the "Gay Nineties."

Author note. *A native Nebraskan who attended the University of Wyoming, Bethene A. Larson has been a resident of Cody, Wyoming since 1962. She is a member of the Big Horn Basin Writers as well as Wyoming Writers. She has had historical articles and poetry published in national, state, and local publications.*

WHEN MY SON COMES HOME
by
Orval Meier

Emma Jessop interrupted her jam making and went to the screen door to escape from the heat of the kitchen for a moment. That's when she spotted the two horsemen cantering through the sun splashed morning. They were still a half mile distant, and their dark figures bobbed like corks in the sea of sagebrush and yucca.

She glanced upward at the nearby mountains rising like jagged, rock knuckles above the brown Wyoming foothills. Their grandeur undulated slightly in the midsummer heatwaves. A toasted breeze flowed around her chunky body and blew a lock of her graying hair across her eyes, momentarily shutting off her vision. She brushed it back with a pudgy, work-used hand, and with the same motion, dabbed at droplets of sweat on her brow.

As she watched the riders lope closer, an indefinable clutch of anxiety stirred within her, for they seemed sinister even at a distance. She shrugged the thought away. I've never been afraid of strangers before she chastized herself, so why should I be this time? I've seen all kinds come and go along this road leading up to the mountains. However, cold fingers of apprehension spread through her. She dried her hands on her long, printed, cotton apron, surprised to find them shaking slightly.

She stepped quickly to the stone fireplace and took down the heavy rifle from above the mantel. The feel of its familiar hardness somewhat reassured her. She checked the load, closed the breech, and set the weapon behind the open door where it would be within easy reach if needed. She returned to the strawberry jam simmering in the iron pot on the stove, but she carefully watched the approaching men through the kitchen window.

A great longing enveloped her. She wished that Sam had not gone to Cheyenne. He knew how to handle riders who came to their door, for he'd taken care of strangers and trouble throughout their thirty seven years of marriage. She could lean on him, safely sheltered by his strength, and if only Clay had stayed home to help them with the ranch! If only . . . nobody would dare mess with her son! Hot tears crept into her eyes as she thought of him. Unfortunately, neither of her men were at home, and she would have to deal with the situation by herself.

The horsemen passed between the corral and the garden, their mounts kicking up white puffs in the July dust. The woman smoothed her apron and tugged at the collar of her blue, calico dress. She had slightly outgrown the garment during the past year, and she wanted to make sure it didn't gap across her ample bosom. She glanced into the mirror hanging by the door and patted at the perspiration on her forehead. The square, care-lined face with deep-set hazel eyes she saw there were framed by brown hair that had begun to salt with gray. She didn't like her late, middle-aged look but had no time to worry about it now. She stepped out onto the small, raised porch to greet the newcomers.

As she ran her eyes over them, she felt another surge of fear. They were a hard looking pair. They were unshaven, crusted with sweat and grime, and the white dust that covered their clothes gave them a spectral look. More than that, they had a sullen, hostile air about them.

One was tall and wire taut, and his lank, black hair straggled down his shoulders like oily twine. He had a long face with a sharp chin and nose, and his green eyes smoldered under half-lowered lids. She judged him to be about thirty.

The other was younger and smaller. Greasy, yellow locks escaped in gnarled tufts from beneath his hat. He fixed her with pale blue eyes that scowled from a round, baby face.

"Mornin'." The taller one touched the brim of his hat and pulled his thin lips back, baring yellowed teeth, in what was meant to be a grin."

"Mornin'," Emma returned, cloaking her uneasiness under politeness. "What can I do for you boys today?"

"We'd like ta water our horses and rest a bit, if yer wouldn't mind." The rider kept his eyes averted.

"Sure," she replied. "Help yourself. The pump's there and the aspens ort to make a good shade from the hot sun. You're welcome to both."

"Much obliged." The man nodded as he and his companion dismounted and stretched their saddle weary bodies. They turned and walked toward the watering trough.

She could not help noticing that the younger one walked with a heavy limp, dragging his left foot awkwardly. He seemed to sense her watching him, for he swung to look at her. His blue eyes, staring through narrowed lids, could have melted glaciers, and she shuddered.

Emma turned quickly and went back into the house to her strawberry jam. She wished that the screen door had a hook on it so that she could fasten it, but it didn't.

As she worked, she paused at the window between the range and the cupboard, holding her can of paraffin. She noticed that the men had unsaddled their horses and put them in the corral. Dismay and dread rose in her. No stranger had ever done that without asking. *When I'm through with my jam, I'd better go have a talk with those two,* she thought. She put her hand behind the door and fingered the rifle. Oh, if only Sam or Clay were home!

Trying to shrug off her mounting fear, she returned to the big stove and finished sealing the jars with the scalding paraffin. As she set the can down, she heard the screen door close softly behind her. She turned to see the tall rider standing just inside. A small cry of surprise almost escaped her, but she composed herself and made her voice sound as calm as she could. "What can I do for you?"

"Yer here all by yerself?" The man made it sound more like a statement than a question.

"Well . . . I . . . that is . . . for a spell," she stalled.

"Where's yer man?"

"Who, Sam? . . . Oh . . . he's . . . well, he's in town for the day. Be back soon. Yes, he and the hired hands will be back soon," she tried to lie convincingly.

"When'd they go?" the man pressed, looking around the room boldly.

"This mornin', early."

There was a short pause. "Funny thing about that, lady. We don't see no fresh tracks goin' out of here nowhere, and we didn't meet a soul on the trail." The man's voice mocked her.

"Well, they did, just the same. Him and the hired hands," she snapped defiantly, as she tried to stop her hands from shaking. "They should be home soon. Now why don't you let me fix you up some grub and some coffee so you can be on your way before they get back. They don't cotton much to strangers hangin' about." She paused as a sneer flashed across the visitor's face.

"Yer man or men don't worry me none, lady." He crossed to the stove and shook the nearly empty coffee pot. Then, reaching into the cupboard and grabbing a mug, he poured some of the dark liquid and tipped it to his lips. "But ya can rustle us up that grub, and make some more coffee too. I like mine hot and black and stout—so strong that ya can float a spoon on it." He sucked noisily at the brew. "So ya fix it like that, hear?"

Anger erupted in Emma like hot lava. "Now see here," she exploded. "Nobody comes into my kitchen and tells me what to do!"

The stranger grinned jaggedly over the rim of the mug. "There's a first time for everything, lady. Ya'll learn."

Her fear vanished, replaced by sudden rage. "You get out of here," she flared. "I'm not fixin' you nothing!" Her mind flashed to the loaded rifle standing behind the door, and she flung herself in that direction. Her hands gripped the cold, metal gun barrel, and she tried to turn it toward her tormenter.

His lithe body was upon her in an instant, twisting and wrenching the weapon away. He slammed his heavy boot heel down on her foot, crushing her instep and sending a thunderbolt of pain ripping through her. She stifled a scream of agony as she crashed backward against the hewn log wall.

"That's jest a samplin' of what ya'll get if ya try a stunt like that agin!" he grated as he ejected the shells from the rifle. "Ya go gettin' foolish with me, and ya'll never see yer old man ner nobody else either." He glowered at her, and the pure venom in his eyes made her throat convulse.

Without taking his eyes from her, the man removed the rifle's bolt and flung it out the door. Then he shoved the useless firearm into a corner. "We'll have that grub now," he commanded.

Although she still smoldered inwardly, the excruciating pain in her foot had drenched all the fight in Emma. She hobbled meekly to the large stove and took out her cast iron frying pan. "You'll be sorry," she muttered to herself, "when my son comes home."

The young stranger shambled into the room. "Ain't no sign of nobody nowhere, Roth," he shrugged. "I looked the whole spread over, too." He pushed his hat back from his dirty, blond hair and gazed at Emma with baleful, blue eyes.

"Well, set yerself down. This here lady's kindly rustlin' us up some grub. Ain't that nice o her?" Roth snickered.

Benton hesitated for a moment than shuffled, stiff legged, to the table. "Much obliged," he murmured, easing himself into a rough-hewn but sturdy, pine chair.

Emma eyed him curiously. "How'd you hurt your leg?"

"Well, we was in Three Forks and . . ."

"Shet up yer mouth, ya idiot," Roth interrupted vehemently. Then turning to Emma, he explained. "Benton here got mistook for somebody he waren't and got hisself plugged. Ain't that right?" He leered at the younger man. Benton nodded and fell silent.

The woman grudgingly served biscuits left over from the day before, salt pork, eggs, and coffee. She limped torturously to the corner of the room and dropped dejectedly into her homemade rocker. She watched Roth take out a large hunting knife and cut up his meat. He stabbed large chunks of it on the knife's point and shoved them into his mouth. As he ate he stared at her from the corner of his eye. A frown creased a furrow between his eyes. Despite the heat and pain, she felt cold and shivery.

She averted her eyes, looking everywhere but at Roth. Then she noticed the large, black revolver hanging at Benton's hip. Her mind raced. If only she could get her hands on that gun! A kaleidoscope of thoughts raced across her vision. Her imagination generated a series of plans—none which seemed workable.

"More coffee." Roth's harsh voice interrupted her.

Coffee! The germ of a plan swirled into her churning mind. If she could somehow throw the pot of scalding liquid into Roth's face, she might be able to snatch the weapon before either of the men recovered from the surprise. She hobbled painfully to the stove, removed the lid from the heavy enameled pot, and turned toward the table.

"And don't get no idee about blistering us with that hot coffee." Roth brandished the ugly knife at her. "Ya may blind me, but I'll find some part of ya with this blade before ya can get away, and . . ." He paused, and a slow grin twisted his face. "Ya won't be a pretty sight when I get through."

"What makes you think she meant to throw it on us?" Benton asked as Emma, feeling defeated, submissively poured the coffee and put the pot back on the stove.

"I been watchin' her. I know what she's thinkin'. She's thinkin' that she can buffalo ya and me and get away. But that ain't gonna work," he growled as he speared a large piece of pork on the end of his knife. He shoveled it into his mouth and chewed ravenously.

"Ain't no use of us stayin' around no more anyway," Benton mumbled through his mouthful. "Her old man'll be comin' home, and we don't need no more trouble. If he's got a hired hand or two with him . . ."

"Yes, we got two," Emma interjected hopefully as she sat down again.

"That's a bunch of hog wash!" Roth spat between chews. "There ain't no hired hands. Ain't no place for them to stay, and there ain't no sign of none. She's lyin'. And as fer as her old man's concerned, my rifle kin take care of him from the window as he comes up the trail." He smiled with malicious anticipation and pushed another load of food into his mouth.

"Well, I don't like it here. Somethin's makin' me darn uneasy."

"Yer always uneasy or yellow-livered scared most er the time," Roth snarled. "I ain't hearin' no more. We been looking fer a place ter hole up, and this looks good ter me."

Benton started to say something but thought better of it and resumed eating.

At that moment there was a shout from the yard. Benton and Roth were on their feet instantly with their revolvers drawn. Crouching low, Roth scuttled to the window and peered out. "Mrs. Jessop, are you there?" a man's voice came again.

"Who is it?" Benton rasped, huddling down beside the table.

"A man on his horse. Git out there on the porch, woman! Send him away. Stay right by the door and talk up so I kin hear ya, an' remember—try anything and yer dead. You and him both." Roth motioned to the woman with his weapon.

Emma rose quickly. "Just a minute," she called as she limped toward the door. She winced at the sight of the big forty-five pointed directly at her midsection with Roth's evil eyes behind it.

"Why, hello, Seth!" She forced a smile and tried to sound cordial as she stepped onto the porch, letting the screen door slam behind her.

The young man astride a big bay eyed her with a friendly stare. "Hello," he returned nonchalantly as he began rolling a cigarette. "I'm on my way up to the old stompin' grounds. Thought I'd stop by and see how you folks were gettin' along."

"Oh, we're . . . fine. Just fine." Emma twisted her face and rolled her eyes toward the two horses in the corral, trying to call the young man's attention to them, but he didn't notice.

She shivered, feeling the large weapon trained on her back. "S . . Sam's in town today." She had to pause to get her voice under control. "Should be back soon, him and the hired hands." She bit her lip, hoping that Seth wouldn't remark that they didn't have hired hands.

The rider finished making his cigarette and lit it. "Sure is hot," he observed, taking a long pull of smoke. "Maybe I could get some water and be on my way."

The woman felt a ripple of panic. She had to warn him of her danger someway. Her mind raced, but nothing clicked. She tossed her head in the direction of the corral again, but Seth gave no visible reaction.

"If I run across that son of yourn, can I tell him anything for you?"

She wanted to scream, "Yes, tell him to come home right now. I need him like I've never needed him before." Instead she swallowed a lump that rose in her throat and said, as calmly as possible, "Tell him that we're fine—that we are living higher than an old red-dog. Ask him to come by soon." She placed heavy emphasis on the 'red-dog', a code for danger in her family.

"Will do," the young man chuckled. "I'll tell him the very next time I run across him." He reined his horse about. "Well, I better go. I'll pick up some water at the well and be on my way. Tell Sam I stopped." He hesitated for a few seconds. "How'd you hurt your foot?"

Emma glanced down at her throbbing, swollen ankle. "Oh," she smiled wanly, "it's just a little sprain. Nothing bad."

"Glad to hear it." The man touched the brim of his hat, wheeled his mount around, and rode toward the well. He quickly filled his canteen and let his horse drink its fill then rode away.

"So long," he called cheerfully over his shoulder. Emma's heart sank as she looked after his receding shape. He hadn't understood one thing that she'd signaled to him. Her shoulders slumped, and tears of disappointment made her stumble as she returned to the kitchen.

"That was good, woman," Roth hissed as he looked out of the window at the departing rider. "Ya do that way all a time, and mebbe nobody'll get hurt."

He holstered his gun and looked sharply at his partner. "We gotta be more careful," he said with a tinge of irritation in his voice. "That dude got clean up here without us seein' him. From now on, one of us'll always be on the lookout. We got ter be a heap more careful." He stood frowning silently for a few moments, then he brightened and turned to Emma. "Now me and Benton'll take some o' that strawberry jam ya got whipped up over there."

"I'm savin' that for my husband and my boy," she flared. "It wasn't made for the likes of you."

"Git it over here, and be quick about it," the man snarled. "I'm gittin' tired a yer sassy ways."

Her foot throbbed, and she wondered if the fierce swelling meant that it was broken. She got up and hobbled painfully to the cabinet, took a jar of the delicate, red preserves, and slammed it on the table between the two men. Roth dug his knife point into the flavorful substance and sampled it gingerly. He went back for a large bite, smacking his lips appreciatively. "Thet's real good," he winked. "Jest like my own Ma used ter make."

Emma, standing by the cupboard, grimaced and snorted loudly. "You had a mother?" She feigned disbelief.

"Course," Roth turned sarcastically. "How else do ya think I got here?"

"I figured a sick buzzard puked on a stump," she spat the words with as much distaste and disdain as she could muster.

The man stopped eating in mid-bite. Slowly he turned his head and focused his full, deadly glare on her. She heard Benton gasp and realized that she had gone too far.

She didn't see the blow coming, for Roth moved with the speed of a cat striking a mouse. As he came up off the chair, his fist struck her cheek just below the eye and slammed her head to one side. She reeled backward, and her shoulders smashed into the cabinet door. Stars sparkled and popped before her, and she grabbed at the wall to keep from collapsing.

"I warned ye twice, woman," he snarled. She felt him grab her arm in a vice grip and vaguely saw his face jammed against hers. "Now

I ain't talkin' no more, ya understand?" Seething rage gritted in his voice.

Emma fought the oblivion that threatened to engulf her. As her mind cleared, she heard Benton laughing—a shrill, high-pitched cackle. "Hey, what's yer name, lady?" he gurgled.

The woman set her mouth stubbornly and looked at the floor, determined to ignore the question. Then Roth's hand snatched her chin, jerking her head up viciously. "The man ast ya somethin'. He expects an answer—now!" His voice came flat and cruel.

"Jessop," she tried to keep from sobbing. "Emma Jessop."

"Well, Mrs. Emma Jessop," Benton chortled. "Yer gonna have a black eye. A real big one. An' if I was ya, I wouldn't be nasty ter Roth here. He'll hurt ya a lot worser next time."

Tears flooded Emma's eyes as the man released her. She sought blindly for her rocking chair and sank heavily into it. "When my son comes home, he'll track you down like the mangy cur you are," she managed to say between tearful convulsions.

"Yeah, sure," Roth sat down and jabbed his knife into the jar of jam, nearly impaling Benton's finger which was already there. He dredged a large serving, sloshed it onto a biscuit, and gorged it into his mouth. "An' yer old man, an' yer hired hand, I mean yer *two* hired hands, an' God Almight, an' anyone else who may come along. Right, pardner?" he roared, slapping his hand on the table as if to wake the young man up.

"That's right. We got ter be real keerful of her kinfolk." Benton joined in the laughter. "I'll be plumb skeered ter sleep jest thinkin' about it."

Roth continued chuckling as he stuffed another hunk of salt pork into his mouth. Emma watched as he gave his full attention to eating, consuming the last morsels and swabbing his plate with a biscuit. With a sigh he cleaned his knife on his filthy trouser leg and leaned back. He stretched languidly, belched and yawned. "I want ter thank ya fer a mighty fine meal, lady—that is, Mrs. Jessop. Me an my friend here sure do appreciate it, don't we, Benton?"

The other nodded vigorous affirmation while picking at a front tooth with his fingernail.

Emma did not respond. Every heartbeat sent a throb of pain pulsing through her foot, and her cheek felt hot and swollen. She only had a half-moon of vision through the puffiness in her left eye. A demanding, overpowering urge to break down and weep caused tears to surge up and distort the world around her. She commanded herself to tighten up; to hide her fear and weakness from them. She bit hard on her lower lip.

At length Roth yawned again and hoisted his lanky body from the creaking chair. "Think I'll go take a nap somewhere. Nothin' like a full belly to make a body drowsy." He peered owlishly around the house. "Benton, ya keep a real close watch on this lady. Make sure she don't try any of her shenanigans. If she does, belt her with yer gun barrel, and keep a lookout on the trail, too. We cain't afford ter have anybody else a slippin' up on us." He shuffled into the bedroom, the only other room in the house, and flopped onto the brightly quilted bed.

"Hey, what about me?" Benton called peevishly after him. "I'm sleepy, too."

"Ya kin sleep later," Roth snapped, then he sighed luxuriantly. "My, my," he crooned. "Real down pillows. Ain't this nice!" He pulled his hat down over his eyes, and a few minutes later, Emma could hear him snoring lustily.

Anger scoured her. The man was lying on her clean bed with his grimy clothes and his horribly dirty boots. She thought ruefully of her newly completed quilt, pieced during many a long hour to form the wide wedding band pattern. All the scraps she had saved over the years had been stitched by her plump, worn hands into a tapestry of her life with Sam. As the colorful stripes twined and encircled each other, so had their existence—the trials, the heartaches, the love, the caring—all now desecrated by that dirty body. She wanted to scream in fury and frustration, but she calmed herself by sitting quietly and smoothing the wrinkles in her apron.

"Emma," she said to herself, "everything is going to be all right. Maybe Clay'll come home." That thought steadied her somewhat, and she decided to turn to the only thing she knew of that would ease worry and fear—work.

"Is it all right if I do the dishes?" she asked Benton who had leaned his chair back against the wall on its two back legs. He had his thumbs hooked in the pockets of his jeans.

"Yeah, go ahead. Jest don't try nothin' with the knives and stuff." His voice was toneless and uninterested.

Emma forced her throbbing body to the polished oak dishwashing table and began sorting through the litter left from the meal.

Benton cleared his throat and cast a quick look toward the bed then turned back. "Say," he said in a loud whisper, "kin I have a bit more of that strawberry jam? I jest got a lick, 'cause he hogged it all fer hisself." He jerked a thumb in Roth's direction. "It's real good."

She gazed at him and realized that underneath the grimy, hard-bitten surface, he was scarcely more than a boy. In spite of her smoldering anger and caged frustration, she suddenly felt sorry for him. Her thoughts flashed to her own son out there somewhere in the wide and lonely world, and she had an urge to draw closer to the youth sitting before her. She nodded, took another warm jar of the preserves and a spoon to the table. Then she got two more biscuits for him. After she had removed the lid and the still limp paraffin, she returned to the dishes.

"Thanks," he murmured as he began to eat.

"I'll bet your mother'd be mighty sorry if she knew what you're doing," she said softly.

Benton looked up, startled. "Why?" he asked, immediately on the defensive.

"You're mixed up with some rough company. That'd worry her terribly, wouldn't it?"

"I ain't got the faintest idee," he grated. "I ain't seen her since I was a little boy, three years old mebbe. She ran away and left me."

"Oh, I'm sorry." Emma responded with genuine concern. "Who raised you?"

"My big sister, my grandma—anybody who'd mind me." A far away look glistened in his eye for a moment.

"Where was your daddy?"

Iron hard coldness sliced through the dreaminess on the boy's face. "Look, lady, I don't know what yer up to, but if yer tryin' to soften me up, ferget it. I don't like all these questions. It don't concern ya. Ya ain't writin' my life's story."

"I'm just trying to help . . ."

"Shet up! Jest shet up!" he gritted. "I hate people meddlin' in my affairs."

Emma wanted to scream at him, to help him understand that he was destroying his young life, but the taut, closed look on his face cut off any further discussion. She clamped her jaws and continued washing dishes while her mind turned to Clay. She finished her chores and limped back to the rocking chair and sat down.

As she rocked gently, her pains seemed to recede like ebbing waters on a lake shore, and she dozed fitfully. Once she awoke and saw Benton sleeping too, but as soon as she stirred, his blue eyes slitted open, watching her with suspicious, catlike interest. The half empty jam jar sat on the table beside him. She drifted back into a troubled slumber.

Suddenly the scuffling of boots scrambling on the planked floor snapped Emma from a dream about Clay. Benton stood by the window, and she noted with surprise that the brilliance and heat of the afternoon had faded into the soft serenity of evening. She had slept longer than she realized.

"Riders comin' fast," the boy called sharply, and she heard Roth's boots hit the oval shaped rag rug in the bedroom. He hustled to the window, his revolver clutched in his hand. Benton drew his weapon too. "There's at least ten of 'em," he breathed.

Roth beckoned to Emma with his free hand. "Git out here," he ordered harshly. "Tell us who they are."

Emma pushed herself to her feet, hobbled gingerly to the screen door and peered out. The distant mountains, crested in clouds of sunset glory, cast long, purple shadows across the muted, evening landscape. Joy flooded through her as she recognized the approaching horsemen. "Oh, thank God!" she half shouted, feeling tears of gratitude and relief sliding from her eyes. "It's Clay . . . and Seth! He did understand my message after all!"

Roth spun on her, a question wrinkling his brow. "Who's Clay and what message?" he demanded.

"It's my son, Clay," she managed through the growing lump in her throat.

Benton looked at her for a long moment. "Clay . . . Clay . . . Jessop," he mouthed the words. Then his eyes opened wide. "Not *the* Clay Jessop?"

"Yes, that's him." Emma could not suppress a half sob.

"You mean the Clay Jessop who shot the men in Deadwood and killed the sheriff at South Pass?"

"Yes, that's my son," she said slowly. "It tears my heart when I hear things like that about him, and I'm not proud of what he does, but at least he don't go around beating up on women." She glared at the two men. "And he does take good care of Pa and me." A heavy sigh escaped her.

Benton blanched visibly and nervously holstered his gun but quickly drew it again. "Clay Jessop is one of the most dangerous men in Wyoming," he gasped turning to Roth. "I tole ya we ort ta leave! I knew we shouldn't stay here!" His voice almost whined. "I don't want nothin' ta do with him. He's a real outlaw, Roth, worsern you ever pretended ta be."

"He only gets mean when he's threatened or angry, like when somebody beats up his mother." Emma couldn't keep the note of triumph from her voice.

"Look," Benton quavered, beseeching her with his eyes. "This waren't my idee. I wanted ta leave, but Roth wouldn't. Remember? An I never hurt ya, not once, did I? Ya tell him that, won't ya?" He holstered his gun again.

The woman felt a surge of half revulsion, half pity for the youth sweep through her. "You didn't try to help me," she snapped.

Roth turned on the boy. "You yellow-bellied coward," he snarled in a low, guttural tone. "Ya ain't got the guts of a . . ." He trailed off, but Emma could see that his hands were shaking and that his pallid face was twisted with fear. "It's all a mistake," he whispered to no one in particular. "Jest a mistake. I'll tell him that. He'll understand how it is when yer on the run."

"I don't think he'll stop to listen now," Emma breathed, feeling a small thrill of exultation. "And those boys he's got with him, they're some of his Robbers' Roost cronies. They won't listen either."

Roth turned toward her, a look of evil cunning warping his visage. "They'll all listen as long as I got one thing," he husked. "They won't do nothin' as long as I got you." He lurched in her direction, his arms outstretched, clutching and grasping.

Emma instinctively shrank backward until she stumbled into the table behind her. She put her hand back to steady herself, and it touched something familiar—the freshly opened strawberry jam. She grasped it and flung it with all the strength she could command. The heavy jar struck Roth flush on the mouth with the sodden sound of mashing flesh.

She threw herself toward the door, sidestepping Benton's lunging clasp. Outside she ran across the porch and down the steps, the wracking pain in her foot nearly forgotten in her fear and desperation.

"Clay! Clay!" she sobbed as she floundered blindly toward the corral where the men were already dismounting with their rifles drawn.

Author note. *Orval Meier, a Sundance resident, has been a member of Wyoming Writers' for five years and was the newsletter editor for 1982-83. He has had two short stories, a magazine article, and several poems published. One of his poems appeared in the Wall Street Journal. Orval has also won prizes and honorable mentions for his work at four Wyoming Writers' workshops.*

LAURA
by
Cynthia Vannoy-Rhoades

Laura Kenny pulled the light sweater around her thin shoulders and slowly pushed open the heavy doors. The sunlight hurt her eyes for a minute, but it felt so good after the stuffy nursing home. She always tried to take a walk, when the weather was warm. After all, at 84, she wasn't sure how many days she had left to enjoy the sunshine.

The sun was warm, but Laura liked having the sweater. It was fall, and the breezes sprung up unexpectedly sometimes.

She walked out to the grassy lawn in front of the home. It was a pretty place, with lawn chairs set up and shade trees, leaves now yellow, here and there. A sprinkler was going in one corner, shooting a crystal spray of water high into the air.

Laura had been here two years, and the homesickness had still not gone away. She missed the tiny cabin in the hills, and had been hurt and sick when her son sold the land and suggested that she go to the nursing home. "It will be better for you, mom." Hank had said. "You'll be with people your own age, and there are people who can take care of you."

"I can take care of myself." She had answered huffily. "I don't need a nursing home."

"It would be best, Mother Kenny." Her daughter-in-law added. "You'll like it there, and Hank and I will come to see you as often as we can. We're afraid that you'll get hurt living up here all by yourself."

Laura had argued some more, but it was really too late. The land and cabin had been sold, the money went to buy Hank a new house, and to pay for Laura's stay here in the home. She received monthly checks from Jake's, her late husband's, social security. She got by.

It was too bad that Jake left the ranch to Hank. Now the land was sold, and he seldom even came to visit Laura in the home . . . Christmas, and sometimes on her birthday in May. At least, that was better than some of the residents, whose families came not at all. Many of the residents could have been dead for all their families seemed to care.

As one man put it, "This here place is just a waiting room for the mortuary." Laura figured that he was about right. Most of us will die here, she thought, our lives used up and over.

Her walk today brought her to the pasture not far from the home, whose fence bordered the nursing home's lawn. It was a large, green pasture, used by the veterinarian hospital nearby for recuperating animal patients. Laura enjoyed watching the livestock that was kept there. They reminded her of her life on the ranch. Mostly there were cattle, this being ranching country, often horses and sometimes sheep or goats. Today, Laura noticed a new arrival to the pasture.

It was a tall, white horse, with fine legs and an intelligent face. Laura noticed that the horse held up one bandaged hind leg carefully, and that the leg above the bandage was crisscrossed with purplish cuts.

"Poor baby," Laura said, looking at the horse. The horse turned its attention to her and hopped painfully over to the fence. Laura patted the soft nose and tangled her gnarled fingers in the horse's coarse mane.

"Poor horse, you're cut up pretty bad, looks like. But you'll get well. You're young, I think, not like me. You'll run again, and be beautiful. You're beautiful now, but I'll bet you look lovely when you run."

The horse, a mare, reminded her of Sadie, a mare she had owned the year after she married Jake, way back some 60 years ago. She remembered the day Jake had come home from the auction, where he planned to buy a milk cow so that young Hank could have fresh milk. He had bought the cow, but had also used up the last of their money for a skinny, half starved foal. Laura didn't protest his decision, although they needed winter clothes for Hank and a store of groceries for the coming winter. The liquid brown eyes of the tiny foal had gone straight to her heart, and she loved it instantly and throughout the winter Hank and the foal shared the warm milk from the cow.

Sadie had repaid them well. She grew tall and strong. Laura remembered training her to saddle, and could catch her anywhere by standing in the pasture and lifting up the apron on her dress, filled with oats, and Sadie would come running. She rode Sadie for many years, riding the range with Jake to gather their small herd of cattle. Those where the good years, the years to remember.

Sadie lived for 28 years when Laura lost her one winter in a blizzard. Jake bought Laura another horse to take Sadie's place. It was a good horse, and Laura rode it for several years, but Sadie had been special.

Laura was so lost in her reminiscing that the horse almost upset her when it pushed against her gently with its nose. Laura petted the horse some more before turning and continuing her walk around the yard.

"I'll come back tomorrow," she told the horse. "I'll try to find an apple for you."

The next day when Laura went to visit her new friend, the horse seemed to be waiting for her and came to the fence eagerly when Laura walked up. Laura had begged an apple from the home's dietitian, a small, round man who had looked at her curiously but had asked no questions.

"Here, girl, I brought you a goodie." Laura held the apple flat out on her palm, and the mare daintily picked it off and crunched into it, dripping juice on Laura's palm. The apple gone, the mare seemed content to hang her head over the fence for petting.

"Good, wasn't it?" Laura asked the horse. "I'll get you another one tomorrow."

People driving past the home saw the old woman petting the horse, and one day a newspaper photographer stopped and requested permission to snap their picture as Laura posed, reaching up, stroking the horse's forehead. The next day the picture was featured on the front page of the small local paper, and Laura clipped it out and hung it on the wall above her bed.

A few days later, after rain had kept Laura from her daily visits, she walked back out to visit her friend again, taking her two apples to make up for the neglect. A group of men were standing around the horse, discussing something that Laura couldn't overhear. As she walked up to the fence, the horse, whom she had privately named Sadie, came over, holding her injured leg carefully off the ground. Two of the men left and the third man followed the horse over to the fence.

"Hello," he said pleasantly to Laura.

"Hi. You must be the veterinarian." Laura had often seen him working with the animals. He was young, but he seemed to know what to do.

"Yes, I am. I see you here very day lately. This horse seems to take to you."

"She does," Laura answered, stroking the horse's nose. "I like her, too. Is she getting better?"

The man's face turned sad and grave, and he looked off towards the nearby mountains before answering.

"I hate to tell you this. I hate to tell anyone. This is a fine horse, a valuable horse, and this shouldn't happen. She isn't getting better, the infection is too widespread. The men who were just here are her owners. They agreed to let me put her down."

Laura felt a lump in her throat. "Isn't there anything you can do for her?"

"I'm sorry. This is the kindest thing we can do," the vet said gently.

Laura turned away for a minute, so the vet wouldn't see the tears in her eyes. "I understand," she said. "It's the only thing you can do."

She petted the horse's head one last time. The beautiful, soft eyes looked at her, and the warm lips nibbled on her hand.

"Goodbye, Sadie," she said, turning to go. The horse stood, watching her.

During the next few weeks, Laura often looked across the lawn to the vet's pasture, wishing that she could see the white horse. but there were only cows and sheep. She hadn't realized until now how much the visits to the horse had come to mean to her.

In the evenings before she fell asleep, she would gaze at the newspaper clipping on the wall, remembering the horse's warm nose on her hand. Then she would fall asleep and dream of her youth, when she would ride like the wind across the plains.

Winter came early, making itself known with snow flurries and day long storms. Thanksgiving came and went with a special dinner for residents in the home.

Winter depressed Laura, as it always had. No walks now, with zero temperatures. Laura looked out the window, trying not to make white horses out of the swirling snow.

She was feeling her 84 years acutely, and there seemed to be nothing left in the world for an old woman, dependent upon nurses and aides to take care of her.

Christmas came and Laura opened and read her few cards, mostly from old friends: A letter came from Hank, enclosed in a Christmas card with a jolly elf on the cover, saying they wouldn't be up to visit her this Christmas.

"Money is tight this year, Ma," the letter read. "Cindy needed braces, and the gas prices are so high. Maybe we can make it at Easter. Here's a check for $50.00. Hope you have a merry Christmas." Laura laid the letter aside. She would like to see Cindy, her granddaughter, but it was a long trip, 300 miles or more. Still, she was disheartened that they couldn't come.

Most of the other residents received similar excuses from children and relatives, so they made their own Christmas; buying each other small trinkets on the day when the senior citizen bus stopped by to take them downtown to shop. Laura used the $50.00 for a warm sweater and a bathrobe to wear on the cold nights and picked up several small presents.

She enjoyed the Christmas party put on by the staff on Christmas Eve, when they sang carols, ate goodies, and drank hot cocoa and apple cider. In the morning would be the gift exchange, with gaily wrapped packages sitting under the tree.

After calling good nights to the other people, Laura went to her room, wanting to read a little in the new *Ideals* magazine that a friend had sent. Opening the door to her room, she saw a large square, slightly flat package, wrapped for Christmas.

The card on it read, "To Laura, from her friends here."

Hastily, and with trembling fingers, Laura undid the strings and tape, too impatient to wait until morning. Inside was a framed painting of an old woman, stroking the forehead of a beautiful white horse.

It was a copy, beautifully done, of the newspaper clipping—only much more alive and colorful. The horse seemed almost ready to turn her head and step out of the painting into real life. She was touched by the beauty and thoughtfulness of the gift. "Maybe it isn't so bad here after all. I have friends and I'm still alive and healthy. I wish I could thank all of them, right now."

She didn't realize she had spoken aloud until she heard a knock on the door and shuffling in the hallway.

She opened the door, and it seemed as if everyone in the home was trying to crowd inside at once.

"Do you like it? Isn't it beautiful? What do you think of it?" The voices tripped over each other.

"I love it. I love you, all of you. I have never had a lovelier Christmas present. It's very beautiful." Her voice broke, then she smiled. "I'm going to hang it right here where I can look at it every morning when I wake up," she told them, hanging the picture at the foot of her bed.

Later, after everyone was gone, Laura left the overhead light on, so the painting of the old woman and the horse was the last thing she saw before closing her eyes.

Author note. *Cynthia Vannoy-Rhoades began writing at the age of 14, and has been writing for about 12 years now. She has written for the Wyoming Outdoor Reporter, The Casper Star Tribune, the Tri-State Livestock News, Wyoming Stockman Farmer, The Country Journal, and two articles appeared in the book, This is Wyoming - Listen.*

THE BOY IN THE BLUE RAINCOAT
by
LaVonne Olds Quinn

The first time I noticed him was when I was fishing the Platte River one night in the fog and the mist, carrying my six pack of beer with me for company. My girl had just walked out on me, the rent was past due, and all I had for a little ray of hope was the rumor that the trout were still taking the bait in the Platte.

I sat there, huddled over my fishing pole, my thoughts as foggy and gloomy as the weather, when I heard a voice behind me say, "Man, are you doin' any good?"

I looked around and he was standing there, tall and thin and predatory looking, like a hawk perched on a telephone pole, watching for a rabbit. But what I noticed first about him was the raincoat he wore. It was longer than he was. It hugged his skinny shanks like it was glued on him, but what was most noticeable about the raincoat was its color. It was a bright, metallic blue and it shone in the dusk along the river as though it were lit up from the inside with some weird, artificial lighting.

"What are you doing here?" I asked him. "You look like you ought to be up at the gym practicing basketball with the Varsity."

"Oh, I blew that off a long time ago," the boy commented. He thrust a skinny hand at me. "My name's Billy. What's your handle?"

"Steve." It suddenly occurred to me that this lanky, over friendly kid belonged to an age group that was supposed to account for a major amount of the nation's crime and maybe he really was a hawk watching for a rabbit and he had me cast as the rabbit.

"What are you up to, anyway?" I asked. "I'm just gettin' in a little solitary night fishing. If I'd wanted company, I'd have asked somebody along."

The boy smiled, and it was like somebody'd turned on a light switch back of his smile and lit up his whole face. "You're all right, sir," he said. "You're really all right."

"Look." I was embarrassed now. "You don't have to make me feel like an old man. I'm twenty-six years old, not over six or seven years older than you."

"I'm nineteen."

"Old enough to drink legally, huh?"

"Just turned nineteen. I'll take a beer if you don't like to drink alone."

"I guess maybe it depends on the company I'm keeping, but yeah—all of a sudden, I don't want to drink alone."

I felt good. A full moon was floating out of the clouds and shining on the river and I could see it reflected again on the shiny surface of the boy's blue raincoat. My beer tasted like champagne, and I stood as tall as Laramie Peak, and I felt like I didn't have a care in the world. I felt like the boy in the blue raincoat was—was—what the hell was the matter with me, anyway? This kid was no angel in disguise, come bringing tidings of heaven on earth. This was just a lanky, puny looking nineteen year old boy who should be warming his bones in front of a fireplace, instead of down here soaking wet beside the Platte River.

I waited while he drained a second bottle of beer, then I said, "How long has it been since you've eaten? I've got a roast that Meg cooked and left in the fridge just before she moved out."

Later on, I sat and watched him putting away what was left of that roast and washing it down with a pot of my rank, black coffee. Again I felt that strange, warm glow, just like I was a rich man, instead of a poor jerk who'd joined the unemployed a few weeks ago and hadn't even been able to hang on to his woman.

"Well, guess I'll go back to the park," the kid said, after he'd eaten—picking his teeth and watching the flames in my fireplace. I threw some more wood on the fire.

"It gets pretty cold in the park at night," I commented. "Sack out on the sofa if you'd like."

What the hell! Had I lost my mind? This gawky kid could steal me blind and run out into the night, afterwards. Worse yet, he could creep into my bedroom and bash my head in while I lay sleeping. Who knew what kind of a kook he might be?

"Naw, I think I'll wander on. The park's kind of nice at night. You can listen to the river splashing against the bank, and once in a while a big granddaddy trout does a dance up in the air, and comes back down again in the water. It's kind of peaceful." He walked to the door, saluted me with his fingers held out in some kind of odd way and walked on down the street.

The next day I found a job. It wasn't much, just a temporary thing; answering the telephone for a company that was selling some kind of novelty merchandise. But it was better than nothing, and it would help me catch up on my rent.

Meg didn't show up, but by now, I was getting kind-of used to my own company.

I saw him again, the boy in the blue raincoat, a couple of nights later down at the Terrybrook Inn. He was talking to a construction worker who lived down the street from me—Ted Hewlitt was the man's name.

Later on, Ted came over and bought me a beer. "Who in hell is that skinny kid?" he asked me. "He looks like a sick hawk, but there's something about him. You know, I was getting ready to have a real jamboree brawl with one of the cowboys who hangs out in this joint and guess what happened?" He shook his head and studied his bottle of beer for a moment. "That puny kid came over and walked real casual-like in between us, just like he hadn't even noticed we were getting ready to fight!"

"So what did you do?"

"What did we do? That's the part you won't believe. All of a sudden I forgot what I'd even wanted to fight about and I guess the cowboy must have, too. We all three ended up drinking a beer together and talking about how the World Series came out!"

"I know where you're coming from," I grinned. "I met him the other night."

"The cowboy?"

"No, Blue Raincoat. He's something else, isn't he?"

A week later, he came back to my house. He looked as hungry as ever and he gulped down a bowl of potato soup and a ham sandwich and washed it down with some more of my black coffee.

"Are you still sleeping in the park?" I asked him.

"Yeah, it's not very cold this time of year. I like trees better than a ceiling over my head and walls around me. Walls give me claustrophobia."

"Don't you have any kind of job?"

"Last summer I worked in a sawmill. Since that folded, I've been picking up some dishwashing at Kelly's Grill."

"How'd you happen to come here? You're not a native son, are you?"

"No, I'm a transplant. My mom died a year ago. My dad never was around. Work prospects dried up, so I drifted out West. Not much better here now, but I like the country. Times, early in the morning, down by the river, the air smells like it did, virgin fresh, when the West was still frontier."

I laughed. "Now, how would you know how the air smelled then?"

He smiled, his strange, lit-up-from-within smile, and peace crept into the room with us like a small, timid animal not yet sure of its welcome.

"You're still welcome to sack out on my sofa, Billy," I told him. I felt strange, using his name. I never had heard his last name.

"Thanks, Steve," he said, "but no thanks. 'Preciate the grub and the company." He vanished into the night and I never saw Billy again.

The next time I heard about him, he'd walked between two winos waving knives at each other in the park and had taken the full brunt of one of the knives in the chest. The wino whose life he'd saved reported the incident to the police and a search was instigated, but to no avail. Billy had disappeared from our town and, apparently, from our lives.

"The wino was goggle-eyed," one of the policemen told me. "He said this kid in the blue raincoat walked coolly in between him and his buddy, took the knife that was meant for him in his own chest, then pulled it out like he was pulling a needle out of his finger and walked out of the park."

About two weeks later, I found a package on my doorstep as I left to go to work. It contained a shabby, faded gray raincoat with a rusty looking spot on the front of it. I knew who'd sent the raincoat. I checked the pockets and found a brief note.

"Dear Steve," the note read, "I'm sending you my raincoat because I don't need it anymore. You won't be able to find me, but take my word for it, I'm happy and well. Wear the raincoat once in a while and think of me. Billy"

I hung the raincoat in my closet and tried to forget the whole thing.

The next morning, I woke up feeling lousy—worse than I'd ever felt in my whole life. Meg still hadn't showed up and I couldn't locate her anywhere. I hated the job I had. It seemed trivial and useless and the future looked like more of the same. I thought about waiting until night, jumping in the Platte River, and ending the whole sorry mess.

I decided to take a walk and try to get my head on straight. I went to my closet and started to put on my old windbreaker. My hand faltered and was still as I looked at the faded raincoat on its hanger.

Following an impulse, I took the raincoat off the hanger and put it on. It fit me like a second skin, even though I was half again as heavy as Billy.

I walked outside on the street. It was very early in the morning, dawn was just breaking, and I was alone. It felt like the dawn of creation, or maybe, in the mood I was in now, more like the morning after a nuclear attack, and me the only sign of life left.

I walked out of town, to the park, and I went down beside the river and I stood there for awhile under the trees. I listened to the trout jumping and I felt the moist, cool air from the river creeping in under my collar, and I breathed the pungent scent of the Platte in all its muddy glory.

Then, gradually, I noticed another sound. A sound so close it seemed to be coming from inside my head—a soft, insistent humming in my ears. As I listened, the humming began to separate into individual sounds; the voices of birds, the rustling of trees, the whirring of insects, the deep-throated chugging of frogs. All these sounds were beginning to form a pattern, a language that I seemed to understand with some new sense organ that I didn't even know I possessed.

The barriers were down and I felt within myself the joy of the bird's winging flight from the trees into the blue sky. I tasted the tantalizing sweetness of the flowers while the bees drank the nectar for their honey. I felt a quick throb of pain as an early morning hawk swooped on an unwary robin. Yet at the same time, a thrill of predatory triumph warmed my blood as the hawk's victory became my own.

Then I felt my breathing growing deeper and more rhythmic. My chest inflated like a hand was inside me, pumping up my tired lungs—filling them with a substance that was lighter and more intoxicating than any ordinary air I had ever breathed could have been. My flesh began to feel very warm and glowed with a heat that was not of the sun, for the morning still held the chill of dawn. The humming in my ears was growing louder. I fell on my knees by the muddy Platte River and bathed my burning face in the flowing water and gradually all the sensations I had been experiencing washed out of me. I was myself again, just Steve. Just another member of the bleeding, sweating human race.

I glanced down at myself and at the raincoat I was still wearing. It was no longer the faded gray color it had been on the hanger. It was blue again—bright, shiny, metallic blue as it had been when Billy was wearing it. Oh, well. No miracle that. Some jewelry took on life and vitality from the warm blood of its wearers.

There was nothing really different about me at all except, maybe, one thing. I knew I'd never really feel alone again.

I walked on home. The dawn broke completely and the world around me was beginning to get back to its normal, workaday self. I hung the blue raincoat back in my closet. I took eggs and a package of bacon out of the fridge and began cooking breakfast. I didn't want to be late to work today. Jobs were too hard to find.

Author note. *A native of Wyoming, LaVonne Olds Quinn was born on a ranch near Douglas, Wyoming. She is a member of the National Writers Club as well as Wyoming Writers.*

SIGNAL FROM SUNDOWN
by
Nancy Ruskowsky

Lights beamed and bobbed throughout the Red Lake area. Although the vehicles seemed to move at random through the night, wobbling across the countryside, they were bent on a purpose—finding their founder.

This was the Cedar Valley Search and Rescue at work; the very group Jim Jackson had established while Sheriff of Greenough County. Six foot Jim had walked through life easy and proud, a man seemingly meant to fill that life with firsts.

He was the firstborn in Johnny Jackson's family, rode the lead team on his dad's twelve horse string, and originated the motorcycle cop position in Cedar Valley. Although he'd been one of the first men on the highway patrol, he wasn't the first man to tickle Elsie Jacob's heart. For forty-seven years though, he knew he was the only one who lived there.

Jimmy had failed to come home for supper. He'd told Elsie at lunch time he was taking a new team out for the afternoon. Buck and Tab were three year old Belgians; a matched pair, perfect team Jim had hoped.

He had taken the truck and his Blue Heeler, Rick, to the old Jones barn where he kept the horses. March 24th, birds fluttered overhead, noisily proclaiming the arrival of an early, early spring. A gentle Chinook warmed the hillsides and the deep rust red of the ancient lake bed looked hungry for the green grass to moisten its dry edges. Intangible smells of fresh rain and new growth were heady perfumes.

At 72, with wavy silver hair, an ever ready handshake to match his easy smile, and an openness that made people eager to be around him, Jim was pursuing his favorite hobby, the horses, with as much energy as ever. Oh, he'd had a round with surgery, but that was a year ago and this was a delightful looking afternoon.

Jim caught the sorrel geldings easily, tempting them with a bucket of grain. With tail thumping impatiently, the dog waited, watching as Jim brushed the horses, talking to them as he worked. When the horses finished their grain, Jim put on the harness.

Hitching them to the wagon, he glanced at the sun, checking the time and mapping his afternoon drive. He'd take the McIntosh Road, cross Sulfur Creek, and wander back in among some of the old deserted cabins.

Rick crouched, ready to leap onto the wagon seat. Jim put his hand up. "No, Rick, not today. These guys are still young and unpredictable. Stay by the truck."

With that, Jim reached down and hugged the Blue Heeler, "You've been a good old dog, Rick." Rick squirmed free of the unaccustomed treatment and readied muscles to leap if Jim changed his mind.

As the dog waited, his master, in levis and a denim shirt, raised a long leg as he stepped onto the spoke, climbing onto the wagon. Jim adjusted the old beat up Stetson, pulled it low over the fading blue eyes, squinted into the sun and turned back to Rick with a snap of his fingers. "I said STAY, Rick!" Rick stayed.

Jim gathered up the lines in long gnarled fingers as Rick laid down in disappointment. The horses headed southwest across Red Lake, bumping onto the ruts of the old McIntosh Road.

The sagebrush had new tips of gray green. Suddenly a bluebird, the first Jim had seen this year, landed on a bush just off the roadway. Jim pulled the team to a stop and just enjoyed.

There hadn't been much snow this winter. Jones Mountain was topped with white and off in the distance, Ptarmigan looked like a diamond dropped in the earth, but here there wasn't even a crystal of ice hidden in the shade.

Jim loved this McIntosh Country. He'd traveled every inch of the state; first as a teamster's helper, his dad's. Later, he'd broke and trained riding horses and sold driving teams.

Life sure had taken its turns. His kids—having Sam working with him as a deputy while he was Sheriff—Don's buying the old homestead. It had been the foundation for a business that had made Don most successful. Now the two girls were back in town with their families, close enough for a daily cup of coffee.

Jim shook his head, clicked to Tab and Buck, and was on his way again. All the fresh air and spring smells must be getting to him. He felt dizzy. He shook his head and as it cleared, went on.

What great weather! It was just this kind of day in '52, they'd got a call at the office about that crazy tourist who went mountain climbing. Jim had called his nephew, Allan, and several of the best mountain men around Cedar Valley. They came as they could and what a team! Getting the poor tourist off that ledge on the mountain where he'd fallen and into the hospital was a beautifully smooth and organized effort. It had made Jim realize a Search and Rescue Unit could be the greatest of assets to his Sheriff's Department. Within a month the group had formed, and had been actively saving lives and improving their abilities ever since.

The very best part of being Sheriff was all those people. Dan, his jailor—they'd run the historical society together. He chuckled. Mostly they had run the big feeds. Pancake breakfasts along a stream for the whole historical bunch on their treks; hamburgers and beans on a rocky crest with memories of homesteaders wafting with the campfire smoke; and steaks grilled at dusk. Contented conversations dwindling into sleep with the sun's fall behind a peak.

Suddenly Jim's mind came back to the present as a coyote leaped through the brush, running full-speed away. Jim lost sight as Tab shied, pulling Buck with him. That, in turn, caused Buck to spook, yanking back towards the road. For a little while even Jim's expert fingers played tough on the lines as he talked soothingly to bring the horses back on the roadway.

Jim felt that dizziness again as scenery melted into wavy, dull gray. Then his eyes cleared, but he could still feel his heart pound. "Tab, Buck! Get back in line."

From there the horses pulled together up toward Sulphur Creek Ridge. A motorcycle roared in the distance, probably some dirt biker. Jim remembered that first Harley Davidson and his first brush with law enforcement. No one had taken him very seriously until he started making some regular arrests. Everyone learned there was no stopping Jim and his 1930 H.D., whether it was across hills like these or on the main street of Cedar Valley.

Jim sighed. He knew this country so well. People didn't realize this land talked if you had sense enough to listen. He kept after his sons to sharpen that hearing—his nephews as well. They all seemed to practice what he taught them. Several were part of the Search and Rescue, keeping their talents fine-tuned with periodic trips to the hills.

Sam specialized in fishing. That boy could find a trout in a dry creek bed—well, almost. Not only did the fish talk to him, he must be able to smell them besides.

Jim could remember gathering up Elsie and the kids for one of those rare quiet days, a fishing trip. He'd teach the boys where the good holes were, but Sam would always say, "That's okay, Dad, you start there. I'll just head upstream." He'd always brought home the supper quicker, too.

A pheasant rose off to the left in a helicopter whirl and whistle, bringing Buck straight up, banging the traces. Jim struggled, berating himself for the mental lapse.

Tab lunged forward leaping into Buck's track, causing the second horse to stumble. Jim stood up, leaning backward hard to pull against the lines, struggling to control the frenzied pair.

That erratic thumping started in his chest again, spreading across his shoulders, weakening his arms. Suddenly, he heard his dad's voice from somewhere long ago, "Remember boy, if your mind slides, your horse'll be too far away to catch when you hit the dust."

Jim's heart pounded loudly in his ears. Still struggling to control the crazy young team, Jim shook his head, trying to hear his father.

"Dad, I've got them. See? I'll get Buck back on the road. Come on, Tab. Aren't they beauties, Dad—just like the ones we always said we'd have? Remember, Dad?"

Then the beating consumed his body and Jim slumped across the seat as the horses, quiet now, turned down a gully, stepping gingerly across an old barbed wire fence that tangled around the wagon wheels. The wire tightened as the horses headed at an angle down the slope. Both Buck and Tab pulled into the traces, just like Jim had taught them.

The old fence posts were pulled from the earth—snapping off under the pressure as the two Belgians continued into the scrub cedar until they were completely tangled—their master no longer encouraging them to "pull harder."

While the Search and Rescue trailed the wagon tracks of their founder, Jim's nephew stopped across the ridge. Pulling off his hat, Allan brushed an arm across his forehead. He had watched the sun drop behind Jones Mountain earlier. Now scanning the area, he tried to sound out the wind. The air seemed to breath.

"Listen, Allan, and you'll hear me. The hills will tell you where I am."

Allan squinted, searching the darkening ridge. His eyes followed the line of the slope down toward Sulphur Creek. He didn't smile. The message he heard was not a happy one. Then, watching the car lights bouncing against the crest, he started down the gully, knowing he would beat the Search and Rescue to the wagon, but not by much.

Author note. *Nancy Ruskowsky started her writing career as a stringer for the Cody Enterprise. Her areas of interest include poetry, fiction, and article writing. She is currently working on a book of non-fiction.*